AMERICAN INDIAN LANGUAGES AND AMERICAN LINGUISTICS

Papers of
The Second Golden Anniversary Symposium
of the Linguistic Society of America,
Held at the University of California, Berkeley,
on November 8 and 9, 1974

Edited by WALLACE L. CHAFE

LISSE
THE PETER DE RIDDER PRESS
1976

ISBN 90 316 0086 5

Printed in Belgium by NICI, Ghent

CONTENTS

PREFACE

This volume is a record of the Second Anniversary Symposium of the Linguistic Society of America, held at the University of California in Berkeley on November 8 and 9, 1974. (The first symposium was held in Amherst in July, the third in New York in December.) Included here are all the papers read at the Symposium, as well as the discussions of those papers prepared by assigned discussants.

The symposium was part of a year-long celebration in which the Linguistic Society of America looked back on its 50-year history, and tried to extrapolate a bit into the future. The symposium at Berkeley, in being devoted to the subject which appears as the title of this volume, was designed to focus on the ways in which the development of linguistics in this country has been influenced by the presence in our midst of Native Americans speaking several hundred diverse languages, many of them seemingly as unlike the languages of Europe as languages can be. It is impossible to know what American linguistics would be like if it had not grown up where it could have firsthand experience of both the range of variation and the degree of commonality among human languages, but without any doubt it would be much different – and certainly much impoverished.

The papers in this collection are remarkably diverse, in both subject matter and style. Such diversity was appropriate to the occasion, reflecting the variety of styles and approaches that have characterized Americanist linguistics. Whatever the reader's interests and tastes, he or she is likely to find something here of value; perhaps some readers will take an interest in the diversity itself. One paper originally planned for the Symposium is missing. Floyd G. Lounsbury of Yale University was to have talked on "Iroquois and Maya: Categories of Grammatical Voice". Illness prevented him from completing the paper or attending the Symposium.

With hindsight it is easy to think of aspects of the interaction between

American Indian languages and American linguistics that were not covered in these papers, or that were only touched on. Place name studies come immediately to mind as just one example. Of course it would have been impossible to say everything in a day and a half; to do the subject justice would in fact call for a large program of research. There is, however, one additional topic that can at least be alluded to in this preface. Sometime before the symposium took place, Michael Silverstein suggested to me that it would be good to include a talk on the particular kind of field experience that Americanists share. It was already too late to add another paper, and it also seemed to me that the subject was an unusually difficult one to cover adequately. Nevertheless, I was struck with the cogency of the suggestion, and wished that at least something could be said about the ways in which linguists have had their outlook on linguistics and languages affected by their contact with peoples and cultures that have been to many of us much more than sources of data.

I remember that a long time ago, as a graduate student who had never seen an Indian outside the movies, 1 arrived on the Cattaraugus Seneca Reservation halfway expecting to find immediately a sedentary informant who would sit down at a table opposite me at 9 a.m. every morning and answer all my questions insightfully in a loud, clear voice, just as had happened in my field methods course at Yale. It didn't happen that way. I won't go into what did happen; everyone has his or her own anecdotes in this area. Suffice it to say that getting used to Indian time and all the rest was unquestionably good for me, not only in a personal but also in a professional way.

In working with an Indian language on its home territory it is hard to avoid becoming something of an ethnologist, or sympathizing with that breakdown of the academic disciplines which classes linguistics as a branch of anthropology. My own experience was fortunate in this respect, since I was privileged to work among people whose own culture is still very much a going concern: a remarkably rich culture, reasonably well documented over a period extending from Cartier's first encounter with it in 1534, and one in which much active interest continues. I found myself involved with a language that was an intimate part of and in-extricable from a complex pattern of ceremonies, songs, dances, myths, beliefs about the world, and habits of daily life. It may be partly because of this experience that I have always found it difficult to accept the notion that "a language is a set of sentences".

Certainly these experiences have influenced our understanding of language as something used by people, and as something that is an integral part of a larger cultural picture. Just how they have affected the things we have done as linguists may be impossible to say in anything more than vague and general terms, but it is something to think about. *ta·ne ˀho wai nẽyo ˀtẽ·ŏ́k, n'õkwa ˀnikŏ́ẽ ˀ* 'And our minds will continue to be so'.

WALLACE L. CHAFE   *University of California, Berkeley*

INTRODUCTORY REMARKS

EINAR HAUGEN

When I opened the first symposium of our Golden Anniversary series in Amherst, Massachusetts, this summer, I pointed out that our tripartite organization of symposia was intended to provide a kind of triangulation in which each symposium zeroes in on one aspect of American linguistics. They are not arbitrary occasions but, as one might expect from good structuralists, a closely interlocking set of explorations from which we may hopefully gain enlightenment and inspiration.

When Leonard Bloomfield tried to answer the question of "Why a Linguistic Society?" in the first issue of *Language* fifty years ago, he specifically mentioned the study of American Indian languages as one area of study for which our society could perform yeoman service. He deplored the almost total lack of funds and organization which led to "direct harm to science" in the case of these languages, "which are disappearing forever, more rapidly than they can be recorded". He saw in them the evidence for his basic view of language, "a similarity, repugnant to the common-sense view, between the languages of highly civilized people and those of savages, a similarity which disregards the use or non-use of writing". And he pointed out the importance of "directly observing and recording human speech", through field work which "has been performed chiefly by the ethnologic-linguistic school".

However old-fashioned some of these formulations may sound to scholars who march to a different drummer these days, and who would rather speculate on the invisible than spy out the informant, it remains true that American Indian languages have been the real grist of American linguistics. We still look to Indianists to keep their ears to the ground and their feet on it. Before the journal *Language* and the Linguistic Society of America, there was an *International Journal of American Linguistics*. What might now be called 'Americanist' linguistics could then be called 'American' linguistics, since there was no other that was more than an offshoot of European linguistics. The latter relationship will be the topic of our third and final symposium at New York in December.

Just twenty years ago there appeared from the press of this university a volume of papers from another symposium on American Indian linguistics, under the chairmanship of Murray Emeneau. Of the six speakers in that symposium, two are also speakers here: Mary Haas and Carl Voegelin. One has passed on, Melville Jacobs, while the remaining three are still active among us, John Howland Rowe, Harry Hoijer, and William Bright. Two other participants, whose papers were not printed here, were A. M. Halpern and R. H. Robins, who has gone on to become one of England's better-known linguists.

The Introduction to that volume emphasized the need for the collection of descriptive data and the importance of much revisiting of the field. Harry Hoijer, who first introduced me to American Indian languages when he visited Wisconsin in the mid-thirties, pointed out the importance of Indian linguistics. Because of the "unique number and diversity of its native idioms" they "provide a laboratory of broad scope for the testing of hypotheses and generalizations". But when he conceded that the study of Indian languages was not "necessary to an understanding of inter-American political and economic problems", we may find that he understated the case. Today the bilingual problems of American Indians and Eskimos have become a clear concern of our national leaders. It is good to see that the needs of native speakers for training in their own languages are being recognized, and at the same time the crucial importance of training Indian linguists who can bring to the study of Indian languages that kind of native competence which alone can illuminate the inmost recesses of language.

THE AMERICANIST TRADITION

DELL HYMES

Berkeley is an obviously appropriate site for this symposium. For a generation it has been the most faithful and active center of Americanist research. One has only to point to the many scholars who have been trained here, and to the many monographs they have provided.* And if one looks for precedent for this symposium, one finds it at Berkeley, again in connection with the Linguistic Society not quite a generation ago. The general essay in that earlier symposium by Hoijer, indeed, says much that is valid today, and on the saying of which one could not improve (Hoijer 1954:3-12).

With such precedent, and with so many leading Americanists in the audience (including Mary Haas, and my own first mentor in the field, Carl Voegelin), I cannot but feel presumptuous in speaking on 'the Americanist tradition'. Others here have shaped it more than I. Let me speak not so much with authority, then, as with surmise. Let me consider the sense in which an Americanist tradition can be said to exist, and project a conception of what the tradition ideally might be in relation to the three communities – general linguistics, Americanist studies, Native Americans – that constitute its public and shape its evolution.

In devoting one of its three Golden Anniversary symposia to American Indian languages and American linguistics, our Society may have intended simply to recognize the great part that Americanist work has played in its past. Loyalty to the sources of one's being – 'piety', as Santayana called it – is indeed essential to health, in a profession as in a person. The Americanist tradition has relevance as well to what Santayana (1905:276) called 'spirituality' – concern with the future and with ideal ends, and I shall try to bring out something of that.[1]

---

* In a series which we must hope is not to be stifled fatally by a false economy, insensitive to the unpurchasable respect ana good will built for a Press and its University by such a series.

Work with American Indian languages of course has a history (by now a considerable history); but a *tradition* implies something more, a continuity not only of object, but also of approach. For some scholars, Americanist linguistics may seem to lurch through time, disconnected, diverse, uninformed by tradition. Yet an irreducible minimum of continuity in approach, of values and understanding, stems from the very nature of the materials with which Americanists work. These data are not replaceable, as are laboratory substances and college sophomores. New data adds, and may illuminate, but cannot wholly replace. There must be continuity across generations, simply because some of the work requires informed knowledge of what predecessors did and why and how they did it.

Often this is so because a given document is the only witness, or only extensive witness, to a language, or state or aspect of a language – hence, precious and to be preserved, as all testimony of the working of the human spirit in the shaping of distinctive symbolic form. The maintenance of such material, its renewal in usable form, is an essential contribution to general linguistics, Americanist studies, Native American communities, all three. Americanist linguistics began as philology of people without philologies of their own, intellectually as part of the stream of interest that founded classical, then Oriental, philology, politically in a context of colony and conquest; it cannot escape the responsibility of this history.

The past interacts with the present for reasons internal to technical work as well. Although each new generation in methodology tends to show contempt for data obtained before its advent, scholars may provide old data with new contexts, such that it may help answer new questions. The more we come to know of a language, or group of languages, the more we can learn from what we have. Even a scanty early word list, if carefully interpreted, can play a part (as work of Madison Beeler, for example, demonstrates). Even if a language is recently well documented, early data may uniquely attest etymological connections, semantic change, or bases of present variation and dialect mixture.[2] Languages are in history, and for American Indian languages early data is precious for showing trajectory over time.

Permanent need for philology is not limited to materials that are old. Ample, generally reliable modern works may require checking against original documents.[3] Thus the original materials, even if published, must be preserved and consulted.[4]

These points bring out two respects in which there must be continuity over generations, given the nature of our data as something for which we care (in a dual sense). The safety and state of materials, even in institutional collections, let alone private hands, cannot be taken for granted. Only personal concern can ensure that manuscript material is not irretrievably misfiled, mislaid, or loaned, or that untranscribed wire recordings and tapes do not become useless through lack of use. An active knowledge of the tradition, as to the activities of predecessors, and the disposition of their work, is essential. Further, to use data from an American Indian language commonly is to depend on work of a few scholars, sometimes fundamentally just one. Documentation of Kathlamet Chinook is essentially from work of Boas, of Clackamas Chinook from work of Jacobs, of Takelma from Sapir, of Chitimacha from Swadesh, of Tunica from Haas, of Tonkawa from Hoijer, etc. Knowledge of a language becomes interwoven with knowledge of a scholar, of the pertinent stage of his or her development, and of that of the field. To interpret the materials, one must interpret the context in which they came to exist. The study of predecessors – of their training, models, habits of transcription, relationships with communities and individuals – thus contributes to both the historiography of linguistics and the analysis of languages.[5]

Leading scholars are aware of the points rehearsed here. They are aware as well that what has been said falls short of actuality. In speaking of a continuity intrinsic to materials, I have reflected not actual history, but an ideal. And in stressing the nature of materials as basis for tradition, I have perhaps played into the hands of those who stereotype Americanist work. Let me try to clarify the relation between an Americanist tradition and Americanist materials, adding to the perduring need to use our materials the perduring need to obtain them.

Yakov Malkiel (1964) has said of Romance linguistics that its most distinctive traits may be deduced from an inventory of its characteristic resources. Whereas the ambit and tone of Romance linguistics can be seen as greatly predetermined by *abundance* of material, preserved or accessible, Americanist linguistics might be seen as greatly determined by initial *absence* of material, and difficulty of access to it.

Much of the Americanist tradition does follow from this situation: the languages were unwritten, exotic, many, and diverse. Ways had to be found to record them, to comprehend them, to relate them. There arose a continuing emphasis on accuracy and salvage of data, within a national culture largely indifferent. The emphasis has been sustained, given the continuing disproportion in number between workers and languages, and recurrent advances in knowledge and method that have motivated return to the same languages, so long as possible. (I have alluded to the frequent disdain of one generation for work of its predecessors.[6] The complement, in part the source, of such disdain has been the need to obtain new materials to help to answer new questions.)

Americanist linguistics, in sum, has looked to the field and the present, more than it has looked to archives and the past. Energies have had to be concentrated on providing data, a task shadowed from the outset by ceaseless decimation of speakers of the languages. Here is the element of truth in the common stereotype of the tradition (and of the anthropological and structural linguistics associated with it).

There follows from all this the importance of field work. What does *not* follow is any single relation between the obtaining of data and the purposes the data is to answer, or the uses to which it is put. There follows no single relation between need to obtain data and kind of data preferred, the sector of language given precedence, the mode of analysis practiced, or academic or intellectual context of interpretation. It is worth remembering that the sanest, most constructive nineteenth-century scholar to interest himself in Indian languages was Whitney, who had no field work with them, and that first-hand collection of data did not prevent Powell and Brinton from misinterpreting languages in terms of received evolutionary and typological ideas far more grossly. If Barton, Jefferson, and Powell sought word lists, while missionaries and Boas sought grammars; if Boas analyzed grammatical categories as central, while some successors focussed on phonology as fundamental; if Sapir developed analysis of aspect, grading, and other semantic features about 1930, while Bloomfield developed immediate constituents; if Swadesh and Pike insisted on use of meaning in description, while Harris sought to avoid it; then the fact that all had done first-hand work with Native American languages cannot explain their differences.

To interpret the course and variety of Americanist work, one must have recourse to what Malkiel called "other powerful determining factors" (1964:671): the specific state reached by a subdiscipline, the matrix of culture that gave it birth and sheltered it, the impact of major leaders. Had descriptive techniques, recording devices, analytic theory developed at a more rapid pace, or earlier in time, in relation to the exploration and conquest of North America and the resulting linguacide, Americanist linguistics would be far different. Had the nineteenth century United States been more French or even British in cultural tradition; had anthropology and linguistics remained so much the province of Western naturalists and Eastern Wasps as to exclude the infusion of German intellectual tradition and liberalism brought by Boas, Sapir, Lowie, Kroeber, Radin, and others; had Indo-European training and Americanist field work come together in a sustained way before Sapir and Bloomfield; had Boas been disinterested in languages as a key to cultural theory; had Sapir or Bloomfield, or both, remained Germanists; had Sapir been able to train students at Berkeley from 1917; had any Native American community been able to support, or insist on support for, study of its own language before recent years; had these and any of a variety of other factors been otherwise, the field would be significantly otherwise as well. What we have, what we know, and what we need to obtain and to know are functions of the interaction of cultural, institutional, and personal factors.

The point is important, because Americanist (and American anthropological and structural) linguistics often has been explained away in terms of materials alone. The importance of the materials gives such explanation enough truth to make it especially dangerous.[7] The evolution of the Americanist tradition, past and prospective, can be better understood if we consider the extent to which the reverse of the stereotype is true. To a great extent, the materials have not determined the scholarship; rather, the scholarship has determined the materials.

We need to know far more than we do about the history of this scholarship. Fortunately, the number of serious and useful studies has grown considerably in recent years. Let me simply mention, alphabetically, work of Darnell (1967, 1969, 1971a, 1971b, 1974), Darnell and Sherzer (1971), Haas (1969a, 1969b), Hanzeli (1969), Hoijer (1973), Hymes (1963, 1970, 1971, 1973), Landar (1975), Rowe (1974), Stocking (1974a, 1974b), and Wells (1974). The main task of positive history has been, and continues to be, *to describe and explain the selective use, and creation, of the resources for the study of American Indian languages.* Much remains to be done. Perhaps some linguists will be attracted to the work by the sheer shock of discovering how false is the current cliché that the nature of the work can be deduced from the nature of the language situation itself. The sheer discovery that the relations between materials and scholars are diverse, and significantly so, may attract research. In any case, I should like now to generalize from the diversity of this relationship, and to state an ideal conception of the Americanist tradition. The reference point of the ideal is indeed the material of the subject, but its comprehensiveness allows for the varied factors that have shaped and will continue to shape its development. An ideal conception might be formulated in these terms: *to know all that can be known about, and by means of, Native American languages.*

With regard to the past, the definition provides scope that is natural to understanding of materials themselves, as an aspect of linguistics, and to explanation of the work which the materials reflect, as an aspect of historiography. What one wants to know about Native American languages, what one wants to know by means of the languages, what information one uses – these parameters have defined a history of considerable change and variation. In particular, the relation of Americanist linguistics to its major constituencies has shown notable change. Study of Native American languages has sometimes been central to general linguistics, sometimes marginal; it has been central to American ethnology for some, not so for others; it has never yet been central to Native American communities themselves, but that time may be coming. Certainly there is a notable change from nineteenth-century writers (Barton, Pickering, Whitney, Brinton) in all of whose pages the Indians are by convention collectively extinct or about to become so, to Boas, for whom Charles Cultee, George Hunt, and Henry Tate are title-page collaborators, to those linguists today who are retained, even paid, by Indian communities.

With regard to the present, the definition has most of all an important corollary: *use all there is to use.* That is, use, therefore get, fresh data whenever possible; marshall data already extant wherever relevant; employ ideas from whatever discipline and source if helpful. The study of Native American languages is ideally an integration of a plurality of modes of work, disciplines, and orientations.[8]

With regard to the future (and as a perspective on the whole of the tradition), the ideal definition implies a comprehensive continuity that is far from being realized. The definition suggests that the materials of the field, far from having wholly determined the scholarship, *have not determined it enough.* The scholarship has seldom been responsive to the materials for their own sake. So much is this the case that today there is perhaps not a single language for which the extant information has been assembled, critically assessed, and made available in an integrated form. Not one. New data continue to be added, and that is essential; old materials are used by specialists, for specific studies; but critical editions of texts, comprehensive dictionaries integrating all vocabularies, lucid grammatical handbooks, systematic guides to languages, language families, language areas – these expectable, indispensable instruments hardly exist. Only a small part of what can be known about Native American languages, and by means of them, can be known now. The basic tools are not in working order.

The prompt, proper answer to this account is that there has not been the support necessary. That is indeed true, but not in itself the whole of the matter. More scholars and dollars are required, but are not in themselves enough. Institutional bases of continuity are essential, and few exist.[9] It ought to be embarrassing, shocking, that there is not a minimum of one chair in Native American languages at each of the state universities. (I am not sure that there is one such chair in the entire country.) There ought to be Institutes of Native American Languages, venerable Institutes that would now be celebrating or approaching their centennials. The scandal of the lack of institutionalization for the Americanist tradition does reflect public attitudes and policies; but it perhaps reflects also a limitation of our own. The continuity of the tradition has depended far too much, far too long, on feats of individual dedication. Most of us have not thought we could aspire to establish the subject in its own right, as a matter of right. Apart from great individual accomplishments, then, such as those of Franz Boas and Mary Haas, attention to the work has depended too much on the waxing and waning of interest in it in the three primary constituencies (general linguistics, ethnology, Native American communities). Until recently the first two, the scholarly communities, have had by far the major role. It may be that only now, when Native American communities become actively involved in shaping their own cultural policies and provide a political constituency for the work, that public support of institutionalization will grow.

To base the work of the tradition on work of Native American scholars and communities as much as possible is the fundamental challenge now and for the future. Many problems are entailed, but it may be only on this basis that Americanist linguistics can realize its potentiality as an object of study in its own right.

In sum, determination of the work by the nature of the materials is not a shackle to be escaped, but an aspiration to be realized. Success may depend on acceptance of a responsibility to the materials because they represent languages that are 'American', not simply in the sense of pertaining to a hemisphere or country, but in the sense of pertaining to members of our own communities, both local and scholarly, in which the languages and the materials retain social function – if not that of personal or religious communication, then that of ancestral heritage and source of identity. The Americanist tradition, having begun as the study of languages of a fading past and far west, will find fruition as the study of the languages of citizens.

Let me anticipate the consequences of such a fruition by way of conclusion.

When one considers the study of language from the standpoint of Native
American *communities*, topics come into view that might otherwise seem
peripheral. The first, most far-reaching consequence of looking at
matters from this standpoint is to extend the tradition to encompass the
full range of sociolinguistic inquiry. Let me just mention salient topics:
Indian norms for English; norms and etiquette of speaking (independent
of the language in question); norms of language use originating outside
Indian communities, but which affect Indian lives; verbal repertoire and
the specialization of languages to particular functions; language obso-
lescence, maintenance, standardization, and revival; the relation of a
community to an ancestral language no longer in use; the role of members of a community in research on their languages, used and ancestral.[10]
    From this standpoint, Americanist linguistic research is not only a
concern for something with roots in the past, but a concern for something
that broaches all the major issues as to the place of language in the society
at large. Quite in contrast to common stereotype, Americanist linguistic
research has the opportunity to be something of a prototype for a broad-
based linguistics of the future. It can become a prototype of a linguistics
that is a community science as well as an academic discipline.
    It may be easier to extend the topical scope of the field than to meet the
challenge of changed relationships to the communities whose languages
and language problems define the field. There is first of all the residue of
colonial relations. Native American communities typically find that
knowledge about their languages, as well as about their cultures, is
stored in archives, libraries, and heads distant from them and sometimes
closed to them. A year or two ago Deni Leonard posed to me the question:
what would one see if one took a map of Native American communities,
and superposed on it a map showing the locations of scholars who know
about the languages of those communities? I could only reflect on the
fact that such a demonstration would show Wasco in central Oregon and
Washington on the first map, and in Chicago and Philadelphia on the
second. A good many linguists are working to overcome these synchronic
discontinuities, but we all know that much much more remains to be
done.
    A sense of responsibility to communities entails a revitalization of the
Bloomfieldian concern for the state of linguistic knowledge in the general
society. Members of Indian communities often suffer from the misin-

formation and misconceptions about language provided them by the schools and persons to which they have access. (They may have been led to believe, for example, that to write an Indian language is to 'put it into English'.) The kind of crusade regarding naive American 'folk-linguistics', which Bloomfield waged, is more than ever needed now. The costs to Native Americans themselves for lack of it are sometimes high. Let us put an end to the irony of scholars travelling great distances, even across oceans, to learn about a language from speakers some of whom have been persuaded to think of it as inferior or worthless.

Responsibility to communities entails an active sense of audiences who are not linguists. It is difficult not to write for the professional reference group to which one belongs, and from which one needs recognition and support, but it is increasingly necessary. To do so goes against the deepset grain of terse elegance so admired in linguistics, a stylistic norm that is part of what has attracted many people to the field; and it goes against the widespread assumption in the academy that something ordinary people can understand cannot be good. Nevertheless, new styles and genres of communication must be developed. Here again, Bloomfield is perhaps the great example to emulate. It is of course not possible to avoid all technical concepts and terms, but it may be surprising to find how much can be made clear, and stated accurately, with sparing use of them. Americanists who master modes of exposition that can be useful to Native Americans may encounter neglect or active disdain from their colleagues, especially from linguists, among whom elitist attitudes have been pervasive. Nevertheless, it is a price one must be prepared to pay.

Practical work has specific demands and costs, but it will in fact be prerequisite to most future field work, and some younger scholars would not want it otherwise. This union of theory and practice, enforced by Native American communities, may indeed provide new depth and richness.

The relation of Americanist linguistics to ethnology will mirror the situation just described. The kinds of contribution that linguistic work can make to sociocultural understanding will be enlarged and enhanced, but at the same time mediated by the relation to Native American communities. If we think of this relation as 'ethnolinguistic', then the established modes of ethnolinguistic inquiry have an opportunity to flourish as never before. Broadly speaking, ethnological interest in linguistic work has had two main concerns, classification and interpretation. Of the four modes of classification of languages, and means of speech –

genetic, areal, typological, functional – only the genetic has had sustained progress in recent years. Much remains to be learned by means of it, but much awaits revival of areal work as well.[11] Typological study, both linguistic and ethnolinguistic,[12] and functional, sociolinguistic classification, have hardly begun to be pursued in a thoroughgoing way, but are likely to have special interest in the future, the one having to do with the ways in which the languages, as symbolic forms, have shaped and been shaped by Indian cultures, and the other having to do with the role of the languages still used in Indian life. By classification, let it be added, I understand a step that leads to explanation, the two being interdependent.

The interpretation of culture through linguistic data has far from reached its potential contribution. Much of the kind of work that can be done involves vocabulary – place names, personal names and titles, the terminologies of various activities – and such work has been shunted aside during the development of formal models of language structure. It has seemed the concern of the antiquarian or ethnologist, but not of the linguist. Much of what Native Americans wish from scholarship, however, as to their own traditions and sometimes rights (as attested for fishing places by sitenames, for example) involves analysis of vocabulary. This is one of the respects in which Native American concerns may enrich the effective scope of the field. The mode of cultural interpretation most actively pursued today is interpretation of texts. Lévi-Strauss has made the world aware of riches hidden in the old unwieldy volumes of the Jesup North Pacific Expedition, and BAE. Much more remains to be disclosed: structure and meaning that can be found only through close control of the language of the texts. Although much of the poetics is lost, much remains to be recaptured. Such work is a prime example of service both to scholarship and to Native American communities themselves. Often the narrative tradition has been disrupted, and scholarship is necessary to bring to life again the oral artistry hidden in old print.[13] Not that it should be assumed that oral artistry disappears with disuse of an aboriginal language. Traditional style may remain vital, and be appreciated and studied, in English. Such study may contribute to contemporary schooling and education, and may illuminate older materials as well. The norms implicit in native language texts are commonly both aesthetic and moral,[14] and current judgments of the propriety of form and conduct may shed unexpected light on texts generations old.

From a community-oriented standpoint, it would be reasonable to attend to the creative work in verbal art going on now.

If one includes the literary uses of language in our field of concern, as did Boas, then what has been done so far is likely to seem only prologue to a vast expansion of attention in the decade ahead.

A base in Native American communities is likely to strengthen the relation of Americanist linguistics to general linguistics. The relation has waxed and waned, as the perceived significance of structural diversity in language has waxed and waned. A virtue of the perspective sketched here is that it makes inescapable the two-sided nature of explanation of language. From the standpoint of a Native American community, one must be concerned to explain not only what Hopi, say, is like in virtue of being a language, but also with what it is in virtue of being the language of the Hopi.

Some may think that the Americanist tradition seized one pole of this duality, the particularistic pole, leaving the universalistic pole to be grasped and developed by Chomskyan generative grammar. Nothing could be further from the truth. The first great mission of Americanist linguistics under Boas was to establish universality. Sapir gave the egalitarian thrust of the work its most memorable expression, from a typological standpoint, when he wrote "When it comes to linguistic form, Plato walks with the Macedonian swineherd, Confucius with the head-hunting savage of Assam (1921:235).[15] The Americanist tradition did, and does, stress the need for an inductive, cross-cultural basis for validity of universals, and cultivates respect for the contours and spirit of the particular language itself; but there are signs that languages themselves are imposing some of this respect anew.

We touch here on the one philosophical orientation which may be said to be inherent in the Americanist tradition. The orientation does not derive automatically from concern with the object of study, and it has not been present always and everywhere. It derives from the German intellectual tradition in which so many major scholars have been rooted. Nor has the orientation been always what we would make of it today. Throughout much of the nineteenth century it regarded American Indian languages as a whole as one type; respect for specific individuality was as gross as a hemisphere and an evolutionary stage. What is noteworthy is that the error was purged toward the end of the century and beginning of the next by men rooted in the same tradition, who applied its concern for inner form at the proper level, that of specific languages, and who did so informed by far closer knowledge of specific languages. Universality was insisted upon, as against cultural prejudice and evolutionary stereotype, but the preferred mode of investiga-

tion of universal properties, beyond the apparent ones, was typological.

This preference for a typologically oriented general linguistics derives,
I believe, from a certain view of the relation between particular and
general in the human sphere. The philosopher Ernst Cassirer has explained the view by contrast to that of Spinoza. For Spinoza, particularity
was limitation, and uniqueness of personality the polar opposite of the
infinity of God and nature. To remain bound in uniqueness was necessarily to be in danger of anthropocentrism and anthropomorphism.
In contrast, Cassirer (1961: 24-25) says:

The neo-humanism of Goethe, Herder, and Humboldt calls for a different
union. To them, the Spinozistic thesis, that definition is limitation, is valid
only where it applies to external limitation, such as the form given to an
object by a force not its own. But within the free sphere of one's personality
such checking heightens personality; it truly acquires form only by forming
itself. Consequently, though we are obliged to recognize in the definition of
personality a limitation, when compared to the infinite being of God and
nature, we are also obliged to acknowledge, and to come to know intimately,
that this very shaping of one's personality is a genuine and underived power.
   Every universal in the sphere of culture, whether discovered in language,
art, religion, or philosophy, is as individual as it is universal. For in this
sphere we perceive the universal only within the actuality of the particular;
only in it can the cultural universal find its actualization, its realization as a
cultural universal.

Cassirer goes on to discuss the way in which Wilhelm von Humboldt has
developed this basic thesis with particular reference to language in
the famous preface to his study of the Kawi language (1836). Cassirer
states (25):

As historian and philosopher of history Humboldt held firmly to this fundamental insight and found new support and proof of it. All historical life is
nationally conditioned and limited; but in this very conditioning, indeed, by
virtue of it, it exemplifies the universality, the unbroken oneness, of the human
race.

And he adds (27): "None of the systems of historical determinism which
we have studied has conceived the principle of individuality with such
depth and clarity."

One might paraphrase this orientation by saying that in the sphere of
human cultural life (including language), universality is fundamentally
a matter of function, rather than of specific form. The creativity and
resultant diversity of cultural and personal ways of life rests in the work-

ing of a universal power, but a power using particular means to particular ends.

It was the accomplishment of Boasian analytic grammar and of the generation of Kroeber, Sapir, Lowie, Radin, and others, to establish such an orientation toward American Indian cultures and languages; to demonstrate the respect in which they embodied the powers universal to man, and at the same time the experience and creativity specific to particular peoples, as against a priori prejudice and rash generalization of whatever kind. If I had to state one philosophical position as 'the' position of the Americanist tradition, I would state this. And I would add that it seems a position consonant with the orientation of Native American cultures themselves.

From this standpoint, the contribution of Americanist linguistics to general linguistics will continue to depend on the importance of testing and discovering generalizations through knowledge of languages originally unwritten and exotic, and still manifold and diverse. There is a further contribution as well. Like Romance linguistics, Americanist linguistics can serve as witness to the claims for relative autonomy of a distinctive subfield. It can serve particularly well within our own society as a reminder of the just claims of a valued body of material for continuous devotion, as against the recurrent claims of a particular approach to be temporary 'king of the mountain' of linguistics as a whole. There is much interest now in the notion of scientific paradigm, as a model for understanding disciplines. Americanist linguistics shows the importance of being able to think, and work, in terms of a scholarly tradition.[16]

In sum, the Americanist tradition has value far beyond that of an object of proper piety. Its implicit aspirations have yet to be fully realized, and its greatest and most comprehensive accomplishments may lie ahead: the collective, chosen work of present and coming generations.

University of Pennsylvania

REFERENCES

Albo, X. 1973. The future of the oppressed languages in the Andes. Paper presented at the IXth International Congress of Anthropological and Ethnological Sciences, Chicago.

Barber, C. G. 1973. Trilingualism in an Arizona Yaqui village. Bilingualism in the Southwest, ed. by P. R. Turner, 295-318. Tucson: University of Arizona Press.

Basso, K. 1970. To give up on words: Silence in the Western Apache culture. Southwestern Journal of Anthropology 26.213-30.

Cassirer, E. 1961. The Logic of the Humanities. New Haven: Yale University Press. Translated by C. S. Howe from Zur Logik der Kulturwissenschaften, Göteborg 1942.

Curtis, E. 1911. The North American Indian. New York.

Darnell, R. 1967. Daniel Garrison Brinton: An Intellectual Biography. M. A. thesis, University of Pennsylvania.

—. 1969. The Development of American Anthropology, 1880-1920: From the Bureau of American Ethnology to Franz Boas. Ph. D. dissertation, University of Pennsylvania.

—. 1971a. The Powell classification of American Indian languages. Papers in Linguistics 4.71-110.

—. 1971b. The revision of the Powell classification. Papers in Linguistics 4.233-57.

—. 1971c The bilingual speech community: A Cree example. Linguistic Diversity in Canadian Society, ed. by R. Darnell, 155-172. Edmonton: Linguistic Research.

—, ed. 1974. Readings in the History of Anthropology. New York: Harper and Row.

—, and J. F. Sherzer. 1971. Areal linguistic studies in North America: A historical perspective. International Journal of American Linguistics 37.20-28.

Frachtenberg, L. J. 1920. Alsea texts and myths. Bureau of American Ethnology, Bulletin 67, Washington D.C.

Goddard, I. 1973. Philological approaches to the study of North American Indian languages: Documents and documentation. Current Trends in Linguistics 10.727-47. The Hague: Mouton.

Golla, V. 1973. Northwest California Renaissance: The Hupa language teaching program. Paper presented at the XIIth Conference on American Indian languages, American Anthropological Association 1973 annual meeting.

Gossen, G. H. 1974. Chamulas in the World of the Sun: Time and Space in a Maya Oral Tradition. Cambridge: Harvard University Press.

Haas, M. R. 1967. On the relations of Tonkawa. Studies in Southwestern Ethnolinguistics, ed. by D. Hymes (with W. Bittle). The Hague: Mouton.

—. 1969a. Grammar or lexicon? The American Indian side of the question from Duponceau to Powell. International Journal of American Linguistics 35.239-55.

—. 1969b. 'Exclusive' and 'Inclusive': A look at early usage. International Journal of American Linguistics 35.1-6.

Hale, K. 1973. Some questions about anthropological linguistics: The role of native knowledge. Reinventing Anthropology, ed. by D. Hymes, 382-97. New York: Pantheon.

Hanzeli, V. E. 1969. Missionary linguistics in New France: A study of seventeenth- and eighteenth-century descriptions of American Indian languages. Janua Linguarum, series maior, 29. The Hague: Mouton.

Hill, J. 1973. Language death, contact, and evolution. Paper presented at the IXth International Congress of Anthropological and Ethnological Sciences, Chicago.

Hoijer, H. 1954. Some problems of American Indian linguistic research. Papers from the Symposium on American Indian Linguistics held at Berkeley July 7, 1951 (University of California Publications in Linguistics 10.1-68), 3-12.

—. 1973. History of American Indian linguistics. Current Trends in Linguistics 10.657-76. The Hague: Mouton.

Hymes, D. 1961. On typology of cognitive styles in language. Anthropological Linguistics 3:1.22-54.

—. 1963. Notes towards a history of linguistic anthropology. Anthropological Linguistics 5:1.59-103.

—. 1965. Some North Pacific Coast poems: A problem in anthropological philology. American Anthropologist 67.316-41.

—. 1966. Some points of Siuslaw phonology. International Journal of American Linguistics 32.328-42.

—. 1967. Interpretation of a Tonkawa paradigm. Studies in Southwestern Ethnolinguistics, ed. by D. Hymes. The Hague: Mouton.

—. 1968. The 'wife' who 'goes out' like a man: Reinterpretation of a Clackamas Chinook myth. Social Science Information 7:3.173-99.

—. 1970. Linguistic method in ethnography. Method and Theory in Linguistics, ed. by P. L. Garvin, 249-311. The Hague: Mouton.

—. 1971. Morris Swadesh: From the first 'Yale School' to world prehistory. The Origin and Diversification of Language, by Morris Swadesh, ed. by J. Sherzer, 228-70. Chicago: Aldine.

—. 1973. Lexicostatistics and glottochronology in the nineteenth century (with notes toward a general history). Lexicostatistics in Genetic Linguistics, ed. by I. Dyen, 122-76. The Hague: Mouton.

—. 1974a. Breakthrough into performance. Folklore and Communication, ed. by K. Goldstein and D. Ben-Amos. The Hague: Mouton.

—, ed. 1974b. Studies in the History of Linguistics. Bloomington: Indiana University Press.

—, and J. Fought. 1975. American Structuralism. Current Trends in Linguistics 13. The Hague: Mouton.

Hymes, V. 1974. The ethnography of intuitions at Warm Springs. LACUS II, ed. by P. Reich. Columbia, S. Carolina: Hornbeam Press.

Humboldt, W. von. 1836. Über die Kawisprache auf der Insel Java, nebst einer Einleitung über die Verschiedenheit des menschlichen Sprachbaues und ihren Einfluss auf die geistige Entwicklung des Menschengeschlechts. Berlin.

Landar, H. 1975. Native North America. Current Trends in Linguistics 13. The Hague: Mouton.

Leap, W. 1973. Language pluralism in a Southwestern Pueblo: Some comments on Isletan English. Bilingualism in the Southwest, ed. by P. R. Turner, 274-94. Tucson: University of Arizona Press.

—. 1974. On grammaticality in Native American English: The evidence from Isleta. International Journal of the Sociology of Language 2.79-90.

Malkiel, Y. 1964. Distinctive traits of Romance linguistics. Language in Culture and Society, ed. by D. Hymes, 671-88. New York: Harper and Row.

Nader, L. 1973. Up the anthropologist – Perspectives gained from studying up. Reinventing Anthropology, ed. by D. Hymes, 284-311. New York: Pantheon.

Philips, S. U. 1972. Participant structures and communicative competence: Warm Springs children in community and classroom. Function of Language in the Classroom, ed. by C. Cazden, V. John, and D. Hymes, 370-94. New York: Teachers College Press.

Rowe, J. H. 1974. Sixteenth and Seventeenth Century Grammars. Studies in the History of Linguistics, ed. by D. Hymes, 361-79. Bloomington: Indiana University Press.

Santayana, G. 1905. Reason in Religion. New York: Charles Scribner's Sons.

Sapir, E. 1909. Wishram Texts. New York: American Ethnological Society.

—. 1921. Language. New York: Harcourt, Brace.

Sherzer, J., and R. Bauman. 1972. Areal studies and culture history: Language as a key to the historical study of culture contact. Southwestern Journal of Anthropology 28.131-52.

Simpson, L. 1973. The deserted boy. Paper presented at the 1973 annual meeting of the American Folklore Society.

Spier, L., and E. Sapir. 1930. Wishram Ethnography. University of Washington
    Publications in Anthropology 3:3.151-300.
Spolsky, B., and J. Kari. 1974. Apachean language maintenance. IJSL 2.91-100.
Stocking, G. W., Jr. 1974a. The Boas plan for the study of American Indian languages.
    Studies in the History of Linguistics, ed. by D. Hymes, 454-84. Bloomington:
    Indiana University Press.
—. 1974b. The Shaping of American Anthropology, 1883-1911: A Franz Boas
    Reader. New York: Basic Books.
Swadesh, M. 1948. Sociologic notes on obsolescent languages. International Journal
    of American Linguistics 14.226-35.
—. 1954. Comments to Stanley Newman "American Indian linguistics in the South-
    west". American Anthropologist 56.639-42.
Troike, R. 1967. Tonkawa and Coahuilteco. Studies in Southwestern Ethnolinguistics,
    ed. by D. Hymes (with W. Bittle). The Hague: Mouton.
Wells, R. 1974. Phonemics in the nineteenth century, 1876-1900. Studies in the
    History of Linguistics, ed. by D. Hymes, 434-53. Bloomington: Indiana University
    Press
Whitney, W. D. 1875. The Life and Growth of Language. New York.

NOTES

[1] For Santayana (1905), 'piety' and 'spirituality' are the two complementary motives
of rational religion. An anniversary, as a ceremonial occasion, does call for a bit of
the 'public religion' of a field, especially when one has been asked (as I have been)
for something 'philosophical', so I hope the reference will not seem inappropriate.
[2] Thus the Powell schedule vocabulary of Wasco, obtained in 1885 by Jeremiah
Curtin, attests as common Chinookan a Penutian cognate for 'pelican'; records forms
and metaphors for features of aboriginal dwellings since forgotten; indicates that the
word for 'horse' was once an extension from 'dog'; etc. The 1884 vocabularies in the
Alsea and Yakona dialects, obtained by J. Owen Dorsey, will make possible control
of possible dialect levelling in Alsean material subsequently collected by Sapir, Frachtenberg, Jacobs, and Harrington. Since in the published lexicon Frachtenberg (1920)
transposed Dorsey's material into his own orthography without indicating which
forms came from Dorsey, it is necessary to go back to Dorsey's own manuscript
(preserved in the Smithsonian).
[3] In comparing Sapir's Wishram Texts (1909) with his field notebooks, I have found
two cases in which, because the narrative apparently had seemed slightly garbled,
Sapir reordered forms for the published record. An analysis of narrative structure
has found motivation for the originally recorded order. See Hymes (1973, 1974a).
[4] Cf. Goddard (1973) for telling examples and an excellent general treatment of
philological assessment of data.
[5] The need to study individual scholars in this way is suggested at the end of Hymes
(1966).
[6] There have been at least two generations in the regard. A linguist exploiting
Hoijer's Tonkawa material for the sake of an issue raised within a Chomskyan framework recently complained that the data did not answer all his questions. That the
original work was done in the 1920s, forty years before, in the infancy of phonology
and morphology, and a reasonable lexicon of some scope, from the last few speakers,
had been a considerable task; that without Hoijer's labors in central Texas there would
have been nothing for later armchair use at all – such thoughts seem not to have oc-
curred. (For different opinion cf. Haas 1967:318, Troike 1967:323, 330, and Hymes
1967:276.) At a 1961 conference Chomsky referred to early materials in American

Indian languages as 'false' (not as limited or incomplete, as I had characterized them).

Such an attitude is not unique to a generation of analysts that works with the principle of transformational derivations. A preceding generation could feel the same way about material obtained without benefit of the principle of phonemicization. I have heard such remarks from several of them, and recently, having sent a copy of Kroeber's Yokuts dialect survey to one senior scholar, because of published attention on his part to Yokuts, was thanked, but nevertheless with serious question as to the utility of the word lists: "Kroeber, however brilliant, was doing this work without benefit of the phonemic principle, which renders his transcriptions virtually unusable." Both linguists and anthropologists have sometimes scorned data from non-professionals (cf. the observations of Morris Swadesh 1954 on this problem). The treatment of Wishram Chinook calendrical names in the one published ethnography (Spier and Sapir 1930) is almost incredible, given the data available in Curtis (1911). (The author of the treatment must be Spier; Sapir would have seen that the Clackamas names (p. 209) are not 'abstract', but analyzable in large part, and in one or two cases merely orthographically disguised variants of Wasco names.)

7   The stereotype of a tradition determined by the exigencies of field work with little known languages is so widespread in textbooks and historiographic writings as to constitute a cliché. Americanist work, American structuralism, and American linguistic anthropology obviously have been closely connected, but none of them can be reduced to a determination by field work. The discovered *content* of Native American languages has had a great impact, but the process of inquiry has greatly varied. Current stereotypes about the process do not reflect direct acquaintance with the tradition and the interplay of field work and other factors within it, but rather reflect a reaction to the ideology dominant among some American linguists in the 1940s. In that decade an image of the anthropological tradition under Boas, Sapir, and Bloomfield was joined with a methodological doctrine derived from certain aspects of Bloomfield's work by the first generation to develop an autonomous academic discipline, associated with wholly general models of linguistic structure. The crystallization of outlook among some leaders of the 1940s has been projected onto the past as a whole. The actual history of American linguistics as related to 'American structuralism' is considered in some detail by Hymes and Fought (1975).

8   Notice that the definition provides no permanent pride of place for field work. Indeed, field work steadily decreases in importance in two respects: (a) from the standpoint of the field as a whole, as the proportion of languages for which field work is possible decreases; (b) from the standpoint of individual languages, as the proportion of what can be newly learned in the field to what can be learned from data already in hand decreases (or falls to zero). In general, field work is one step, or moment, in research, and over time has become less often the first step. Fieldwork is more and more often to be justified as a step following upon analysis, or recognition of a new problem, such that new data is seen to be needed. None of this dimishes the importance of field work where new data *is* needed, or where there is need for salvage or community service. The true situation does make the statement of purpose inside the cover of the International Journal of American Linguistics seem curious: "The functions of the Conference are, first, to discuss matters of common interest to linguists and anthropologists who do field work with American Indian languages; and secondly to pool information on opportunities for publication, and on the sources of subsidy for field work and publication" (see, e.g., IJAL 49(3) (1974)). If taken seriously, the statement implies that an American Indian language ceases to be of interest to the Conference on the day that it ceases to be available for field work. Scholars who do comparative reconstruction, historical analysis, philological interpretation of texts and meanings, or who work with American Indian languages through data obtained by others, are excluded. Field work is implied to be an end

in itself; once published, the use to which it is put is not of interest. Such a statement, officially made in the only journal of the subject, capitulates to those who would reduce a major chapter in the intellectual history of linguistics and anthropology to the gathering of data. It disgraces the purposes to which the great figures of the tradition have worked, and should be changed.

9   The Survey of California Indian Languages, made possible by Murray B. Emeneau and Mary Haas, is one of the important few. The contribution of the American Philosophical Society, through its Library and its Phillips Fund, and of the Smithsonian Institution, should be specially noted too.

10   As instances of the study of such topics, let me mention Leap (1973, 1974), Philips (1972), Basso (1970), Barber (1973), Darnell (1971c), Swadesh (1948), Hill (1973), Golla (1973), Spolsky and Kari (1974), Albo (1973), Hale (1973), V. Hymes (1974). The genres, styles, and norms of non-Indian languages that affect Indian lives have been little studied, whether in regard to Indian communities or otherwise. In general, attention has been given to minority communities in terms of the ways in which in which they are different, and so present a problem for the institutions of the established order. There has been little study of the way in which the established order is a problem for the minorities, and indeed for people generally, except with regard to schooling (on which see Philips, cited above). On the general problem see Nader (1973).

11   Cf. Darnell and Sherzer (1971) and Sherzer and Bauman (1972).

12   Cf. Hymes (1961).

13   Cf. Hymes (1965, 1968).

14   This point is stressed by Gossen (1974).

15   Cf. Whitney (1875). Both statements are at the end of chapters. The attention to universals and theory in the Americanist tradition is discussed in Hymes and Fought (1975). Let me observe that not only does Sapir's sentence contain several well-placed internal parallelisms of assonance and consonance (*come* : for*m*, -*donian* : -*hunting*, *swine* : *savage*, herd : head, and the near rhyme of the stressed, enclosing phrase endings (form : -sam), but also that the two long, parallel phrases count almost as alexandrines.

16   The question of 'paradigm' and 'tradition' is discussed in the introduction to Hymes (1974b).

THE AMERICANIST TRADITION

DISCUSSION BY BRUCE RIGSBY

I want to use Dell Hymes' excellent and provocative paper as a background and springboard to a cursory examination of another national tradition that concerns itself with the study of the languages of a dispossessed and oppressed people – the languages of the Native Australians, both Aboriginals and Torres Straits Islanders. Such a leap from America to the Antipodes is not without motivation, I believe, for there are a number of us who are participants in both the Americanist and the Australianist traditions and there are interesting parallels between the two.

This is not the appropriate place to attempt a comprehensive historical review of the Australianist tradition, so I focus upon the work of Americanists who were or are Australianists too. My narrowed scope reflects a quiet pride in our contribution to the Australianist tradition – a tradition which, I must add, is now institutionalized and vigorously pursued by a host of younger workers at the Australian Institute of Aboriginal Studies, at the Australian National University, at Darwin Community College, and at Monash University.

To establish a historical connection between the two national traditions and to invoke the *mana* of our tribal forefathers, we recall that Horatio Hale – who was Franz Boas' immediate major linguistic predecessor in the Pacific Northwest – published grammars of two New South Wales languages in the last century (Hale 1846) and that Alfred Kroeber published in 1923 an early attempt at the classification of Australian languages after working on the Aboriginal vocabulary materials of Edward Curr and others (Kroeber 1923). And a decade ago, Kroeber's student, Carl Voegelin, and Voegelin's students, Kenneth Hale and Geoffrey O'Grady, worked in the same area of Australian genetic classification (Hale 1964, A, B, C, D; O'Grady 1966; O'Grady, Voegelin, and Voegelin 1966). Voegelin tells me that there was continuity of interest in the problems of Australian genetic classification between Kroeber and himself. More recently, Barry Alpher (1974), a student of

Charles Hockett, and I (Rigsby 1974) have also done Australian classificatory work.

The Australianist tradition, too, has its philological aspects and an
orientation and commitment to fieldwork that are not unlike our Americanist ones. Hymes has argued that the nature of the American materials
themselves have not determined Americanist scholarship, but rather,
that the opposite relation holds and is to be understood only in the
context of 'other powerful determining factors'. A parallel argument may
be made for Americanist-Australianist work.

As I understand it, one powerful motivation in Kenneth Hale's im-
mense Australian work has been the richness of the Aboriginal language
material for developing points of general phonological, syntactic, and
historical linguistic theory (e.g., Hale 1970, 1973a, 1973b, 1974). On
the other hand, Wick Miller, a student of Mary Haas, worked among
Western Desert-speaking people in Australia to study linguistic varia-
bility and its structuring by social and cultural factors (Miller 1971a,
1971b). The connections between Miller's Great Basin and Australian
work are obvious – "Diggers and Doggers" is the title of a recent article
(Gould, Fowler, and Fowler 1972) that labels the native peoples of the
two areas in parallel linguistic form. And Michael Silverstein's present
fieldwork in the Kimberleys with Worora – an accusative island set in a
sea of ergativity – shows both a concern for the general theory of case
and for the interface of linguistics and ethnography *via* a powerful notion
of pragmatic meaning.

The contributions of Americanist-Australianist work have tended more
towards general linguistics than towards ethnology, but I expect to see the
situation reversed in the years to come as our language-in-culture theory
takes form. However, Kenneth Hale's unpublished work on kin and
section nomenclatures (Hale E), on the indexing of kinship dimensions
in Lardil and Aranda complex noun phrases (Hale 1966), and on the
Walbiri 'upside-down' language (Hale 1971) cannot go unmentioned.
As well, two more of Hale's papers – one on the need for transformational rules in an adequate Lardil grammar (Hale 1965) and the other
on number systems and relative clauses in Aboriginal languages (Hale
1975 – have served to dispel some popular notions of the primitive
character of Aboriginal languages. Recall what Joshua Whatmough
(1956: 52-53) wrote about the 'archaic' character of Aranda structure in
Language: A Modern Synthesis and there is an immediate parallel between Hale on Aboriginal languages and Archibald Hill (1952) on the
Cherokee verb forms for washing.

Like its Americanist counterpart, the Australianist tradition is now presented with the challenge and the opportunity of developing new relationships to the native communities that have provided it with the primary resources it has made into its intellectual capital and stock-in-trade. Australianists have responded both on a personal level, which varies with individuals and situations, and on an institutional level. A notable example of the former may be seen in the collegial relationship of Terry Klokeid, a Canadian student of Hale, O'Grady, and Laurence Thompson, and Ephraim Bani, a Torres Straits Islander grammarian, that has resulted in a number of meaty papers (Bani 1974, Bani and Klokeid 1971, Klokeid 1974a, 1974b) and in Bani's move into the state school on Thursday Island as an instructor in the Western Torres Straits Island language. And on the institutional level the Australians have recently staffed and organized a School of Australian Linguistics for training Native Australian language specialists at Darwin Community College. Our colleague, Barry Alpher, has emigrated to join the staff of the School of Australian Linguistics.

The School of Australian Linguistics in Darwin is just one part of a larger social movement whose overall dimensions and goals remain unclear, but bilingual-bicultural education is now Commonwealth policy in Australia. And with new Commonwealth policy on Aboriginal land rights, there is now a movement of a number of Aboriginal groups off the Reserves in the Northern Territory and North Queensland and back to their home countries – this is known as the 'out-station movement'. It simply is no longer possible politically to use police power to hold unwilling Aboriginal groups on alien Reserve territories. The returned groups will need several years to sort out their affairs, but already several returned groups in the Northern Territory have asked that schools and teachers come to them with bilingual-bicultural programs. It is challenges like these that Australianist anthropologists, educators, and linguists must respond to in a creative and moral manner if we are to know 'all that can be known about and by means of Native Australian languages'.

University of New Mexico

REFERENCES

Alpher, B. 1974. On the genetic subgrouping of the languages of southwestern Cape York Peninsula, Australia. Oceanic Linguistics.

Bani, E. 1974. The language situation in western Torres Strait. Paper presented at the Biennial Meeting of the Australian Institute of Aboriginal Studies, Canberra.

Bani, E., and T. J. Klokeid, eds. 1971. Papers on the Western Island Language of Torres Strait. Submitted as a final report to the Australian Institute of Aboriginal Studies. Dittographed.

Gould, R. A., D. D. Fowler, and C. S. Fowler. 1972. Diggers and doggers: Parallel failures in economic acculturation. Southwestern Journal of Anthropology 28.265-81.

Hale, H. 1846. Ethnology and philology. United States exploring expedition during the years 1838, 1839, 1840, 1841, 1842. Philadelphia: Lea & Blanchard.

Hale, K. 1964. Classification of Northern Paman languages, Cape York Peninsula, Australia: A research report. Oceanic Linguistics 3.248-65.

—. 1965. Australian languages and transformational grammar. Linguistics 16.32-41.

—. 1966. Kinship reflections in syntax: Some Australian languages. Word 22.318-24.

—. 1970. The passive and ergative in language change: The Australian case. Pacific linguistics studieds in honour of Arthur Capell. Pacific linguistics series C. 13. Canberra: Australian National University.

—. 1971. A note on a Walbiri tradition of antonymy. Semantics: An interdisciplinary reader in philosophy, linguistics, and psychology, ed. by D. D. Steinberg and L. A. Jakobovits, 472-82. New York: Cambridge University Press.

—. 1973a Person marking in Walbiri. A festschrift for Morris Halle, ed. by S. R. Anderson and P. Kiparsky, 308-44. New York: Holt, Rinehart and Winston.

—. 1973b. Deep-surface canonical disparities in relation to analysis and change: An Australian example. Current Trends in Linguistics, ed. by T. A. Sebeok, 11.401-58.

—. 1974. The adjoined relative clause in Australia. Paper presented at the Biennial Meeting of the Australian Institute of Aboriginal Studies, Canberra.

—. 1975. Gaps in grammar and culture. Linguistics and anthropology: In honor of C. F. Voegelin, ed. by M. D. Kinkade, K. L. Hale, and O. Werner, 295-315. Lisse: The Peter de Ridder Press.

—. A. Phonological developments in Middle Paman: Wik languages. Unpublished manuscript.

—. B. Attestation in stems (Middle Paman). Unpublished manuscript.

—. C. Other Paman languages (attestations). Unpublished manuscript.

—. D. Attestation. Unpublished manuscript.

—. E. Classroom handouts on Australian kinship. Unpublished manuscript.

Hill, A. 1952. A note on primitive languages. International Journal of American Linguistics 18.172-77.

Klokeid, T. J. 1974a. A note on phonological dialect variation in the Western Torres Strait. Paper presented at the Biennial Meeting of the Australian Institute of Aboriginal Studies, Canberra.

—. 1974b. A case-changing rule in Kala Lagau Langgus. Paper presented at the Biennial Meeting of the Australian Institute of Aboriginal Studies, Canberra.

Kroeber, A. L. 1923. Relationships of the Australian languages. Proceedings of the Royal Society of New South Wales 57.101-17.

Miller, W. R. 1971a. Dialect differentiation in the Western Desert Language. Anthropological Forum 3.61-78.

—. 1971b. A reply to Douglas's comment. Anthropological Forum 3.83-85.

O'Grady, G. N. 1966. Proto-Ngayarda phonology. Oceanic Linguistics 2.71-130.
O'Grady, G. N., and C. F. and F. M. Voegelin (with Appendix by K. L. Hale). 1966. Languages of the world: Indo-Pacific Fascicle six. Anthropological Linguistics 8:2.1-197.
Rigsby, B. 1974. Kuku-Thaypan descriptive and historical phonology. Paper presented at the Biennial Meeting of the Australian Institute of Aboriginal Studies, Canberra.
Whatmough, J. 1956. Language: A modern synthesis. New York: Mentor Books.

THEORETICAL LINGUISTICS IN RELATION TO AMERICAN INDIAN COMMUNITIES[1]

KENNETH HALE

American Indian languages have been the object of scholarly attention for several centuries.[1] But despite the obvious and enormous contribution which American Indian people have made to this scholarship, it is a fact that professional linguistics has failed to engage significant numbers of native speakers of American Indian languages in careers relating to the study of the linguistic structures which they command. The field of American Indian linguistics is dominated by non-Indians. This situation is not only detrimental to the science of linguistics, but it has resulted in critical shortage of native-speaking linguistics personnel for the many language-related educational programs which have developed within American Indian communities and in institutions of higher learning attended by large numbers of American Indian students. There are, therefore, both theoretical and practical considerations which justify an effort to reverse the prevailing situation by eliminating the isolation of American Indian linguistics from the people whose languages constitute its primary data.[2]

It has become increasingly clear in recent years, partly as a result of certain advances in the study of the syntax of English and other amply investigated languages, that many important aspects of linguistic structure are essentially beyond the reach of scholars who are not native speakers of the language they study. Even where insights of great importance have been contributed by non-native speakers – to the study of English, for example – it is possible to argue that the insights are based on intuitions which, in all essential respects, closely approximate those of a native speaker. Linguistic information about the structures of American Indian languages is, with a few exceptions, limited to spheres which are more or less readily accessible to perceptive non-native speakers – that is, to areas which can be studied with a minimal appeal to the native speaker's intuitions. Thus, we have a great deal of excellent information on phonology and morphology, but relatively little on syntax.

And the extent to which success has been enjoyed has depended a great deal on the efficiency of the partnership between a non-native-speaking linguist and a native-speaking informant. For many of the most interesting topics of linguistic research, it is doubtful whether this traditional arrangement, in which the linguistic problem is formulated in one mind and the crucial linguistic intuitions reside in another, can work at all – or, where it appears to work, whether it can be said that the native-speaking informant is not, in fact, functioning as a linguist. The proliferation of research problems concomitant with the growth of linguistic science and the dependency relationship between effective research and a native speaker's control of the data conspire to create a problem of logistics which is greatly reduced if the linguist and the native speaker are the same individual. This does not mean, of course, that linguists should cease to work on languages other than their own – there are certain real scientific advantages to being a somewhat detached student of a language; moreover, there exist a great many languages which, for a variety of historical reasons, will require the attention of non-native-speaking scholars if they are to be documented at all. But a native speaker's command is critical in the linguistic enterprise – the advantages here are greater and of a different nature.

In view of the extraordinary contribution which American Indian languages make to the study of the human linguistic capacity, it seems to me to be essential to the future of the field that the state of affairs which now prevails in American Indian linguistics – i.e., its domination by non-native-speakers – be fundamentally altered; and the most productive use to which we could now put the expertise in American Indian linguistics which has developed over the years would, in my estimation, be in the effort to bring about this change.

A most compelling reason for working toward this change is the increasing need for native-speaking language scholars in contemporary American Indian communities. There are many communities which are, for example, anxious to explore the potential contribution of linguistics to their developing bilingual education programs. They are hampered far less by their own vision of the possibilities than by the unfortunate and unnecessary isolation of linguistics from them. These communities are addressing themselves to a problem which is extremely concrete – namely, that of ensuring that their own cultural and linguistic wealth play a prominent role in the education of their children. They recognize the importance of their languages to this effort and the importance of devising sound programs for the study of their languages in their schools.

Moreover, they realize that there exists a field of inquiry which could be directly relevant to their language programs. An outstanding example of this line of thought is that represented by the Diné Bi'ólta' Association, based at Fort Defiance, Arizona, which, among other things, sponsors summer workshops devoted to the development of materials and the training of teachers for the study of Navajo language and culture in elementary education. This is but one of a growing number of cases in which a community of people has defined a set of concerns which relate in obvious ways to the subject matter included under the rubric of American Indian linguistics. It goes without saying that the people who can best decide the precise relevance of this field of study to the concerns of American Indian communities, and the people who can best decide the appropriate application of language scholarship in addressing these concerns, are members of those very communities. But the prerequisite, of course, is that linguistics become available to the communities in a real sense, i.e., in the form of a capable native-speaking linguistics personnel.

It should be pointed out that there has been a significant mobilization of linguistic expertise around the problem of addressing the enormously varied linguistic needs of particular American Indian communities.[3] To some extent, at least, the isolation of American Indian linguistics from the concrete educational concerns of American Indian people is gradually being overcome, and the involvement of native speakers in careers relating to the study, documentation, and teaching of American Indian languages is slowly increasing. However, there are many serious challenges which this movement faces, not the least of these being the problem of surmounting the essentially bureaucratic obstacles which have been erected both in the course of the professionalization of linguistics and in the course of the development of an educational superstructure which severely constrains the routes of entry into careers relating to the teaching and study of language. But there are strictly linguistic challenges as well, and it is to one of these that I would like to direct my attention here.

American Indian linguistics students with whom I have worked during the past several years have been consistent in their commitment to the ideal that their scholarship should be put to *use* in the service of the communities from which they come. The focus of their concern has typically been upon the question of how linguistic scholarship will be of use in education, particularly in bilingual programs. While it is clear that linguistic expertise has a clear role to play in such areas of 'linguistic technology' as the development of writing systems, language engineering, the compiling of dictionaries, language pedagogy, and the like, it is not so obvious what direct relevance the study of linguistic theory has to particular education programs. I think it is only honest to ask whether theoretical linguistics is a mere luxury from the point of view of a person concerned with the practical application of linguistic scholarship. This question has direct bearing on the issue with which I began this discussion – namely, the importance to linguistic science of engaging speakers of American Indian languages in the advancement of linguistic theory. Their enlistment in this effort will depend, to a significant degree, upon the applicability of linguistic theory to educational programs.

I would like to suggest that theoretical linguistics, far from being an extravagance, does in fact have a concrete practical application in education, granted certain assumptions concerning the academic goals of education in the contemporary world. And I would argue further that a bilingual community could make extremely effective use of theoretical linguistics in defining the overall educational role of the language which predominates among its school-age members.

Let us make the assumption that it is a reasonable goal in modern education to prepare students to enter into fields which make essential use of the methods, concepts, and attitudes of scientific inquiry – i.e., to enable them to gain experience in constructing and articulating abstract explanations for superficially mysterious or contradictory observations. It is difficult to imagine a more effective tool for imparting such a skill than the scientific study of language. Linguistic science has the advantage over other sciences that the data relevant to it are immediately accessible, even to the youngest of students, and it requires virtually no material equipment. Moreover, it enables the student to use his or her native language in activities which offer considerable intellectual challenge, an important requirement in the formal education of young children particularly.

The problem is to design a program of study which will in fact encourage students to take an inquisitive attitude toward their native language, a program which, in so far as possible, will avoid the pitfalls of prescriptivism and blind application of a partially understood formalism belonging to some favored theoretical framework. The point is neither to teach the 'grammar' of a language nor to teach a particular linguistic theory but, rather, to use the linguistic knowledge which students possess as a subject matter of science. The possibility that the study of language might enter into the science curriculum in elementary and secondary education is one which deserves to be taken seriously, in my judgment. And American Indian bilingual education programs may be particularly advantaged in this regard in view of the fact that the role of the local languages involved is not constrained by the weight of formal educational tradition. The role is still being defined and there is ample opportunity for creative invention in designing effective educational programs around language and in developing the appropriate teaching personnel.

I wish to devote the remainder of this paper to a brief discussion of a conceivable program for the study of Navajo by Navajo-speaking students in elementary and secondary schools. This is meant to be a suggestion only, but many of the ideas have grown out of an involvement over a period of three years with a small number of Navajo-speakers engaged in the study of their language.[4]

The program can be thought of as proceeding in roughly three stages: I, early elementary; II, late elementary; III, secondary. I will be concerned here solely with the program as it relates to the study of language as a science. It goes without saying that this is a small part of the total role of language in any school program; it is simply the focus of my attention here.

STAGE I

Students at this level will be involved in acquiring literacy in Navajo; hence, language study at this stage will have to be designed with preliterates and incipient literates in mind. The primary effort at this stage should, I feel, be to encourage students to develop a consciously experimental attitude toward language and to learn to verbalize their observations about it. This might be achieved in large part by means of a wide variety of games and game-like activities which involve children in novel and unusual uses of linguistic form and which enable the teacher to focus their conscious attention on what they are doing with linguistic elements when they engage in linguistic play.

For example, as an initial step in drawing attention to the internal structure of Navajo verb words, a game can be constructed on the model of Lewis Carroll's *Jabberwocky*.[5] Basically, this involves the use of fictitious verb stems (e.g., -*baash* 'to bosh' – meaning, let us say, 'to walk the way a robot does'; or -*keesh* 'to cashe' – 'to fly the way Superman does') in combination with actual Navajo prefix sequences (e.g., *naash*-

baash 'I am boshing around', *nishébáázh* 'I boshed there and back', *ch'ínishbáásh* 'I am boshing out horizontally', and so on). The teacher, having illustrated the meaning of, say, *naashbaash*, might engage the students in dialogue which requires them to use the fictitious verb in forms they have not yet heard (e.g., the teacher, boshing, asks: *ha'át'iish baa naashá* 'what am I doing?', and the students answer: *nanibaash* 'you are boshing around'; or, having boshed out the door, the teacher asks: *ha'át'iish baa niséyá* 'what did I do?', and the students answer: *ch'íníbáázh* 'you boshed out', or the like). Alternatively, the teacher may use puppets or models to illustrate a variety of uses of such fictitious verbs – the possibilities are many. When the students learn to use such verbs and enter into the spirit of the game, which they do rather quickly, their attention can be drawn to the fact that the prefixal portion of the verb changes in the ways which correspond to changes in the situation and its participants. Gradually, a conscious awareness of the meanings contributed by the prefixes can be developed, and, most important, students can be induced to articulate their understanding of what is happening in the verb word. This is essential, since the development of a way of talking about language, a 'terminology', is a fundamental aid in their later work. The particular terminology does not matter; though, clearly, the teacher can help the students to arrive at an efficient one.[6]

The ability to construct articulate generalizations about observed phenomena is an important one to cultivate for the purposes of any scientific inquiry. A great many language games are appropriate for exercising this ability. Navajo is especially well endowed in the area of semantics by virtue of its classificatory verb stems, and any number of games can be constructed which will induce students to state the generalizations which relate, say, the subjects of *sitá* 'a slender stiff object is in position', the instruments implied by the verb form *nidíitḥaal* 'I hit him with an elongated object', or the objects implied by *yishchozh* 'I am eating greens'. The classificatory verb stems are ideal for involving students in the novel and imaginative use of their language. For instance, under normal circumstances it would be incorrect to say *ashkii nidiilá* 'I picked up the boy', because the verb stem which is used implies that the boy is long and flexible, like a rope. The proper way to say it is *ashkii nidiiłtí*, using the verb stem which is appropriate for animate objects. One might, however, create an imaginary world, as in a science fiction story, in which the beings are totally unlike the human beings of our planet. One could then ask students to describe an encounter with these beings. An intelligent but rope-like being might be said to assume a stance more aptly described as *silá* 'a long flexible object is in position' than as *sidá* 'he is sitting', or *sití* 'he is lying down', or *sizí* 'he is standing'; his method of taking hold of an object might be described as *yiyiiloh* 'he ropes it' rather than as *yiyiijih* 'he grasps it'; he might fall the way a rope does *(naadeeł)* rather than the way a human does *(hadaatłíísh)*. A student might even allow himself to imagine that the being's gait should be described by the otherwise non-existent verbal form **naalé* 'he "strings" around' instead of *naaghá* 'he walks around'. In any event, imaginary play of this sort provides an excellent opportunity for students to give and to defend their various opinions about the proper linguistic usage in an entirely novel situation and, thereby, to come to grips in a rather direct way with certain semantic properties of Navajo.

The study of phonology can also begin at this stage. An awareness of the articulatory features of the sounds of one's own language is of considerable potential usefulness to students, not only as preparation for a formal study of the phonological rules which exist in the language, but also as preparation for an intellectual understanding of the principles which underly writing (particularly where the writing system – as the standard Navajo orthography does to some degree – reflects the feature composition of sound segments) and as preparation for the acquisition of the phonology of a second language. An appropriate initial step, it seems to me, would be to lead students to identify the most obvious organs of speech – together with their Navajo names – i.e., the lips, the tongue, the tip of the tongue, the back of the tongue, and so forth; this, in fact, is the foundation of a Navajo phonetic terminology which could be amplified and perfected as students proceed through their elementary schooling. It will be of value, as the study proceeds, to let the students become familiar with representational drawings of the speech organs. This involves, at the beginning, teaching them to identify the lips, teeth, tongue, tongue-tip, etc., in 'x-ray' drawings of the type used by phoneticians. It may take some time to get younger children to the point where they can interpret such drawings with ease, but it can be done; and once this ability is acquired, it will prove to be of tremendous value as their study of phonetics continues. While this basic foundation is being developed, it is possible at the same time to have students begin to pay attention to, and attempt to describe verbally, the movements of the primary articulators (lips and tongue) in speaking. For example, the students could be asked to describe exactly what happens to the lips when one begins to pronounce such words as *mą'ii* 'coyote', *máazo* 'marble', *bááh* 'bread', and other words in their vocabulary which begin with bilabials. Once they are able to describe what happens – i.e., to observe that the lips articulate against one another (*hadaa' ahininílá* or *hadaa' ałch'į' át'é*, or however they choose to express it), they can be taught to recognize this position of articulation in a drawing. And similarly for the other positions of articulation – e.g., the tongue-tip placed behind the upper front teeth, as when one begins to pronounce words like *naadą́ą́'* 'corn', *dibé* 'sheep', and so on. The students should be helped to suggest an appropriate description of the articulation for themselves. In this way, a phonetic vocabulary with which they feel comfortable will be developed. Once students are familiar with the four basic positions of articulation for Navajo consonants, it is possible to construct a simple card game which will help them to become thoroughly comfortable with the idea of thinking of sound in terms of their production. The game involves two sets of cards. One set consists of x-ray pictures for each of the four positions of articulation (say, 5 cards for each, giving a deck of twenty); the other set consists of pictures of objects whose initial consonants represent the positions of articulation (say, thirty to fifty cards). The players (a small number) sit in a circle; each player is dealt a hand of four x-ray cards from a shuffled deck; the picture cards are placed face-down in a pile at the center of the circle. One of the players is chosen to start the game. This player turns the top picture card face-up and places it beside the pile; he then consults his hand of x-ray cards, and if it contains an x-ray picture corresponding to the position of articulation of the initial consonant in the word which the picture card represents, he takes it from his hand and places it face-up next to the picture card. If there are two x-ray cards which correspond to the initial consonant of the picture word, the player can place both of them down; if three, all three; and so on. When he has done this, the next player goes through the same procedure. The object of the game is to get rid of all the x-ray cards in one's hand. The winner of the game is the first player who gets rid of his hand. One can imagine several variations of this game; the students will undoubtedly think of ways of changing it. Perhaps the most productive way to introduce this game to younger students is to teach it first to older children, around ten years of age, and have them teach it to the younger ones. This is a particularly good way to establish a terminology for talking about phonetics to younger children. The older group will, in all probability, have an efficient way of giving oral instructions to the younger group, and a great deal can be built upon the terminology they use.

This game (and variations on it) helps not only to enable students to become familiar with the positions of articulation and the role which the articulators play in speech production, but it also helps to teach the fact that sounds belong to classes – e.g., that /b/ and /m/ belong to the class of 'lip-sounds', that /t/, /d/, and /n/ all belong to the class of 'tongue-tip sounds'; and so forth. Once these observations are made, it is possible to begin to introduce the idea of *manner* of articulation. Students can be asked to think about, and to attempt to describe, the differences between sounds belonging to the same position of articulation – e.g., the difference between /b/ and /m/; the difference between /d/ and /n/, and between /t/ and /d/, and so on. Their descriptions of these differences will suggest an appropriate Navajo terminology to be used in reference to the manner of articulation. It is possible to represent the manners of articulation in the form of x-ray pictures as well, by using an arrow to represent the flow of breath. When this dimension is added, and students become familiar with its role in speech production, the card game can be appropriately modified to incorporate it. And when the students have learned the alphabetic symbols, and have begun writing, the game can be further modified by replacing the picture cards with letter cards. The game would proceed as before, but now the players associate an x-ray card with letters. This will help to teach the association between sounds, thought of in terms of how they are produced, and the conventional letters used to represent them.

These are but a few of many conceivable game-like activities which could be used at this stage to encourage children to manipulate linguistic material, to experiment with it, and, especially, to talk about it with ever increasing precision. The central aim of such activities is to create the attitude that linguistic form and meaning are things which can be consciously observed, to set the scene for the discovery of linguistic problems which require solution – something which the ordinary, everyday use of language rarely does.

STAGE II

The activities of the first stage are designed to make minimal appeal to the skill of writing – in fact, they can be almost exclusively oral. At some point, however, it will be possible to take increasing advantage of

the fact that the students are becoming literate in Navajo. This permits
the use of activities requiring greater concentration and the handling of
larger bodies of data.

The study of the internal structure of Navajo verb words, for example,
can be greatly advanced by means of a form of 'scrabble', using prefixes
(rather than letters) to build words. In fact, just such a game can be used
to introduce students to the idea that verb forms have an underlying
morphophonemic representation which often differs radically from the
form which is actually pronounced. Imagine a version of scrabble in
which players are supplied with chips bearing Navajo prefixes together
with numerical values associated with the frequencies of the prefixes.
The object is to use the chips in constructing well-formed prefix sequences,
in much the same way that words are built in alphabetical scrabble.
In the Navajo version, the player is allowed to supply the stem of the verb
(represented, say, by a blank chip). Assuming that the players are aware
of the meanings of many of the prefixes, from their experiences in earlier
games, the frequent disparity between underlying and surface forms
can be introduced by pointing out that the presence of a particular
meaning in a verb form does not necessarily guarantee the presense of
a prefix of a particular shape – e.g., while 'first person singular object'
is typically *shi-*, as in *shiłhozh* 'he is tickling me', and 'second person
singular subject' is typically *ni-*, as in *niłhozh* 'you are tickling him', the
two together do not give **shiniłhozh*, but rather *shiłhozh* 'you are tickling
me', due to a process sometimes referred to as 'ni-absorption'; and while
'first person singular subject' is typically *sh-*, as in *dishni* 'I say', it does
not appear so in *diskos* 'I cough', due to the process of 'strident assimilation' whereby the underlying laminal is converted to an apical under the
influence of the stem-final /s/. By playing the game in such a way as to
reveal the most straightforward alternations, the teacher can introduce
the notion of phonological rule. And, depending upon the students'
ability to handle this idea, it can be incorporated into the game itself by
granting a player extra credit for constructing an underlying representation removed from the surface form through the intercession of a phonological rule (e.g., as underlying /di-sh-kos/ is related to surface *diskos*).
This would, particularly in the more sophisticated versions of the game,
give students an opportunity to exercise their ability to construct argu-
ments in defense of particular underlying forms.

While the central aim of the first stage is to create in the students an
experimental attitude toward linguistic material, I see the primary focus
of the second stage as being the development of an appreciation of

language as a system of *rules*. Phonology, of course, provides ample illustration of the rule-governed nature of language, but syntax and semantics are particularly rich and readily accessible.

The game-like atmosphere which prevails in the first stage is gradually replaced in the second stage by a more laboratory-like atmosphere in which linguistic material is subjected to intense strain – the easiest way to reveal the existence of a rule is to break it. The use of ill-formed words and sentences, therefore, assumes considerable importance at this point. The general strategy in each instance is to present the students with data which reveal the existence of a rule and to encourage them to articulate the rule for themselves. I will content myself with a single example.

It has been suggested that Navajo possesses a rule whereby a transitive sentence of the form SUBJECT OBJECT *yi*-VERB can, by a process not unlike the passive of English, be converted to the form OBJECT SUBJECT *bi*-VERB.[7] The rule is illustrated by the pair of sentences *łį́į́' dzaanééz yiztał* 'the horse kicked the mule' and *dzaanééz łį́į́' biztał* 'the mule was kicked by the horse'. However, it is a fact about Navajo that this rule cannot apply freely to all transitive sentences. Thus, for example, the sentence *łééchąą'í łeets'aa' yiłnaad* 'the dog is licking the plate' is of the form SUBJECT OBJECT *yi*-VERB, but it cannot be converted to OBJECT SUBJECT *bi*-VERB. In other words, the 'passive' counterpart **łeets'aa' łééchąą'í biłnaad* 'the plate is being licked by the dog' is unacceptable in Navajo. Moreover, there are cases in which the rule *must* apply – thus, the sentence *ashkii tsís'ná bishish* 'the boy was stung by the bee', of the form OBJECT SUBJECT *bi*-VERB, has no acceptable 'active' counterpart of the form SUBJECT OBJECT *yi*-VERB – the form **tsís'ná ashkii yishish* 'the bee stung the boy' is unacceptable. Very roughly, the principle is this. Navajo nominal concepts are ranked, with humans highest and inanimate and abstract entities lowest. The rule applies optionally where the subject and object are equal in rank; it must not apply where the subject outranks the object, and it applies obligatorily where the object outranks the subject. That is to say, in cases of subject-object inequality, the rule applies or does not apply so as to ensure that the higher ranking nominal be in initial, or topic, position. This fact of Navajo provides a coherent problem which students could attempt to solve. They could be presented with well-formed and ill-formed transitive sentences illustrating the rule and asked to try to uncover, and to articulate, the principle which governs its application.

Language is rich in material of this sort, and it is a relatively simple matter to assemble data which will illustrate the operation of rules of grammar. It is important, I feel, to use this material in such a way as to enable students to formulate the principles for themselves. The object here is not to teach a list of rules, but rather to exercise the students' ability to express, as precisely as possible, the generalizations which inhere in the data presented to them.

STAGE III

The primary concern at this stage is to confront students with linguistic problems, particularly problems which illustrate the fact that the 'explanation' of observed contradictions in linguistic data requires the use of abstractions, or theories – i.e., the postulation of a level of linguistic representation and design which cannot be directly observed, only defended on the basis of its success in predicting the observable behavior of linguistic form and meaning. The use of counterexamples assumes great importance in teaching at this stage.

The activities of the earlier stages are meant to prepare students to confront linguistic problems. Assuming that they have achieved some measure of skill in linguistic observation and some degree of comfort with the concept of grammatical rule, they are ready to consider counterexamples.

For example, having observed that a stem-initial fricative is typically voiceless when preceded by another voiceless segment (as in *yishxáád* 'I am shaking it', with stem-initial /x/ instead of the voiced counterpart /gh/ appearing in *nigháád* 'you are shaking it'), students are in a position to appreciate exceptions to this rule (as in *yishghał* 'I am eating it (meat)', with the voiced stem-initial fricative also appearing in *nilghał* 'you are eating it'). And, having observed that where a so-called 'classifier' appears in a second or third person form, it is regularly missing in first person forms (e.g., the classifier *-l-* of *nilghał* is missing from *yishghał*, they are prepared to entertain the possibility that the exceptional forms have an underlying representation which distinguishes them from the regular forms, an underlying representation which in some sense explains their exceptionality (e.g., *yishghał* is underlyingly /yi-sh-l-ghał/; the classifier prevents the devoicing rule from affecting the stem-initial fricative). Examples of this sort lead to a somewhat more abstract conception of linguistic phenomena and give the teacher an opportunity to illustrate what is involved in constructing and defending a theoretical proposal. In this instance, not only is an abstract underlying representation (of first person forms of 1-classifier verbs) involved, but there is a problem of rule-interaction as well (i.e., the rule which deletes the classifier must be related to the devoicing rule in such a way as to prevent the generation of the ill-formed *yishxał instead of the correct yishghał.[8]

The rule of strident assimilation offers an excellent opportunity to explore the abstract nature of the putting together of linguistic forms. While the first person object prefix shi- ordinarily assimitates to si- in siztał 'he kicked me' (<shiztał), it does not do so in shéstał 'it (a missile) struck me'. This is because the relative order positions of the object prefix in the two verb forms are different; in the first, the prefix occupies a position which is relatively closer to the stem than the position it occupies in the second. A strong juncture occurs in the second form while only weak junctures occur in the first – but this is an abstract notion since the junctures are inaudible and since, in terms of the surface representations, the prefix is the same distance from the stem in both forms. The discovery of the relative morpheme order within the Navajo verb word – together with the various phonological effects of relative distance – is itself a challenging activity from which students can learn a great deal.[9]

I will conclude with a syntactic example. Once students have achieved a conscious awareness of the meanings of the semantically more perspicuous verbal prefixes and have come to appreciate the function of rules of agreement (e.g., that sh- 'first singular subject' is construed with the subject shí 'I' in shí naashnish 'I am working'; that da- 'plural' is construed with a plural subject in hastiin dóó ashiiké ndaalnish 'the men and the boys are working'; and the like), they can be faced with observations like the following. The sentence *shí ndaashnish is ill-formed, for reasons which are obvious – the subject is singular, yet the verb contains the plural prefix da-; in other words, the verb form is internally contradictory in that the prefix sh- implies a singular subject while da- implies a plural subject. All of this follows from rules whose existence is obvious to any speaker of Navajo. But there are seeming counterexamples to these rules. Precisely the outlawed verb form appears in sentences like (shí) ashiiké bił ndaashnish 'I am working with the boys', in which the verb agrees in person with the surface subject shí 'I' while agreeing in number jointly with the subject and with the nounphrase of the comitative phrase ashiiké bił 'with the boys'. It is as if, from the point of view of number agreement, the subject were instead the compound nounphrase shí dóó ashiiké (as in shí dóó ashiiké ndeiilnish 'I and the boys are working'). The verb form ndaashnish – as a first person form, and not the homophonous third person perfective – defies the ordinary understanding of the operation of the Navajo agreement rules. But it could be made consistent with them by proposing a somewhat more abstract derivation of comitative sentences than is obvious from their surface form. Suppose, for example, they were derived from sentences with compound subjects by means of a rule which elevates one of the conjuncts to subjecthood in its own right while creating a comitative phrase out of the remainder. If this rule were ordered after number agreement but before person agreement, the existence of the internally inconsistent first person verb form *ndaashnish* would be explained. This particular example could also be used to illustrate the requirement that abstract rules of the type proposed here be independently motivated. By positing the rule which elevates a conjunct to subjecthood, it is possible to explain the existence of such internally inconsistent verb forms as *yish'ash* (with first singular person agreement but a dual stem), appearing in *(shí) ashkii bił yish'ash* 'I am walking with the boy', and *ahiistsą́* (with first singular person agreement together with the reciprocal object prefix *ahi-*), appearing in the well-formed sentence – well-formed in Navajo, but not in English translation – *(shí) ashkii bił ahiistsą́* '*I saw each other with the boy'. Thus, the rule is thrice motivated, by virtue of the fact that it must apply after provisions are made for (1) plural number agreement, (2) nonsingular verb stem selection, and (3) reciprocal objects, all of which require reference to nonsingular subjects. Under the analysis proposed here, the sentences exemplified have compound, hence dual or plural, subjects at their most abstract representation, while at their surface representation, when person agreement applies, they have simple, singular subjects.[10]

I do not wish to insist that the analysis of comitatives proposed here is the correct one – nor would it make sense to insist upon a particular analysis for any such problem. The object in teaching is not to present solutions but to illustrate what is involved in arguing for some solution – in this instance, the argument is based upon the fact that the analysis proposed permits the elimination of an identical exception clause from three distinct statements of agreement (i.e., except in comitative sentences, *da-* is construed with a plural subject; etc.), at the cost, to be sure, of an abstract and somewhat unusual rule. The putative saving may, under further scrutiny, prove to be spurious – but this is the very point of linguistic science; the whole enterprise advances by means of the critical examination (and often the overthrow) of proposed solutions to problems, or through demonstrating that the problems themselves vanish under a more insightful and general conception of the issues involved.

To work out the details of a language study program of the type suggested in the foregoing will, of course, require an enormous amount of energy and talent – regardless of the language for which it is designed. Crucial to the implementation of any such program is the development of a linguistics personnel which has native command of the language studied. It seems to me to be reasonable to give this idea some serious consideration in defining the future direction of the field of American Indian linguistics.

Massachusetts Institute of Technology

REFERENCES

Alvarez, A., and K. Hale. 1970. Toward a manual of Papago grammar: Some phonological terms. International Journal of American Linguistics 36.83-97.

Becenti, L. J., and D. Chee. 1974. Diné bizaad dadiits'a'ígíí naaskaah [The study of Navajo sounds]. Diné Bizaad Náníl'jjh/Navajo Language Review 1.39-51.

Creamer, M. H. 1974. Ranking in Navajo nouns. Diné Bizaad Náníl'jjh/Navajo Language Review 1.29-38.

Hale, K. 1972a. A new perspective on American Indian linguistics and some comments relative to the pueblos. New Perspectives on The Pueblos, ed. by A. Ortiz (including an appendix by A. Alvarez), 87-133. Albuquerque: University of New Mexico Press.

—. 1972b. Some questions about anthropological linguistics: The role of native knowledge. Reinventing Anthropology, ed. by D. Hymes, 382-97. New York: Pantheon.

—. 1972c. Navajo Linguistics III. Unpublished Massachusetts Institute of Technology manuscript, 1-92.

—. 1973a. The role of American Indian linguistics in bilingual education. Bilingualism in the Southwest, ed. by P. R. Turner, 203-225. Tucson: University of Arizona Press.

—. 1973b. A note on subject-object inversion in Navajo. Issues in Linguistics: Papers in Honor of Henry and Renée Kahane, ed. by B. B. Kachru *et al.*, 300-09. Urbana: University of Illinois Press.

Higgins, R. 1971. A dialogue on the Navajo classifier. Massachusetts Institute of Technology manuscript, 1-65. To appear in Diné Bizaad Náníl'jjh/Navajo Language Review.

Kari, J. M. 1973. Navajo verb prefix phonology. Unpublished doctoral dissertation, 1-314. University of New Mexico.

Kaufman, E. 1972. Navajo spatial enclitics: A case for unbounded rightward movement. Massachusetts Institute of Technology manuscript, 1-53. To appear in Linguistic Inquiry.

Platero, P. 1972. Diné Bizaad Bibeehaz'áanii. Unpublished Massachusetts Institute of Technology manuscript, 1-61.

—. 1974a. Strident assimilation in Navajo. Unpublished Massachusetts Institute of Technology manuscript, 1-30.

—. 1974b. The Navajo relative clause. International Journal of American Linguistics 40.202-46.

Sapir, E., and H. Hoijer. 1967. The phonology and morphology of the Navajo language. Berkeley and Los Angeles: University of California Press.
Stanley, R. 1973. Boundaries in phonology. Festschrift for Morris Halle, ed. by S. Anderson and P. Kiparsky, 185-206. New York: Holt, Reinhard and Winston.

NOTES

[1] The work described in this paper was supported in part by the National Institutes of Health (Grant No. 5 PO1 MH13390).

[2] Some of the issues involved here are discussed in Hale (1972a,b) and in Alvarez and Hale (1970).

[3] An appreciation of a part of the work being done in this area can be gained from the pages of the *Conference on American Indian Languages Clearinghouse Newsletter*, edited by James L. Fidelholtz and published by the Center for Applied Linguistics. Recent publications by the Malki Museum Press provide excellent examples of cooperative efforts on the part of linguists and native-speaking language workers.

[4] I am particularly grateful to Paul Platero, Ellavina Perkins, and Lorraine Honie for much valuable discussion of these issues, and to Anita Pfeiffer, Dillon Platero, and Paul Platero for enabling me to participate in workshops sponsored by the Diné Bi'ólta' Association, at which some of the ideas involved were discussed and informally subjected to experimentation.

[5] This, and other game-like activities, are briefly described in Hale 1973a.

[6] For a discussion of a Navajo phonological terminology, see Becenti and Chee (1974); and for a discussion of a Papago phonological terminology, see Alvarez and Hale (1970). Navajo grammatical terminology is developed in Platero (1972).

[7] This rule is briefly discussed in Hale (1973b) and, in more detail, from the point of view of a native-speaker of Navajo, in Creamer (1974).

[8] A pedagogical elaboration of this problem, and of the syntactic problem briefly discussed below, is to be found in Hale (1972c).

[9] For a discussion of the internal structure of the Navajo verb, see Sapir and Hoijer (1967:85-101). Discussions of strident assimilation are to be found there and in Platero (1974a) and in Kari (1973). The role of junctures in the phonology of the Navajo verb word is discussed in Stanley (1973). Roger Higgins (1971) has prepared a pedagogically effective discussion of certain aspects of Navajo verbal phonology in the form of a dialogue between laymen and a linguist.

[10] Several recent papers on Navajo syntax provide a wealth of data which could be used in setting problems of the type used at this stage – among these are Platero (1974b) and Kaufman (1972).

THEORETICAL LINGUISTICS
IN RELATION TO
AMERICAN INDIAN COMMUNITIES

DISCUSSION BY MARGARET LANGDON

As soon as the topic of Ken Hale's presentation at this symposium came to my attention, I was reminded of an early programmatic statement of his which appeared in the *Indian Historian*, in the summer of 1969, entitled "American Indians in Linguistics: A plan and a program". I remember being much impressed with the boldness of his conception, although I must admit that at the time I was somewhat sceptical about the chances of its successful implementation, given the realities of the academic establishment. It is therefore with a great deal of pleasure that I am able to withdraw my scepticism in the face of the genuine success which his ideas have enjoyed in the short period of 5 years since the article just mentioned first appeared. It is clearly a case of an idea whose time had come and which acquired in him an eloquent spokesman. It is worth reviewing today two of the main avenues which Hale suggested in 1969 for providing careers in linguistics for native speakers of American Indian languages, namely, university appointments and research centers. I will selectively illustrate each point from cases I have personal knowledge of in the hope that members of the audience will be so incensed at the omissions that they will supplement my presentation from their own experience in the discussion period. In the area of university appointments, I would like to mention the case of California State University at San Diego, where native American languages are taught by native speakers, in the classroom, at the college level. So far, the Native American Studies program there has offered courses in Lakota Sioux, taught by Mrs. Shirley Murphy, who is attending this symposium, and a Kumeyaay Diegueño course, and a Hopi course is planned for the spring semester. The instructors are remunerated at the appropriate academic level of the institution. In general, state and community colleges appear to be in a favored position in this respect because of their sensitivity to community needs and the greater flexibility of their hiring policies with respect to standard academic credentials. As to Research Centers, the most dramatic

instance is certainly the Alaska Native Language Center, where feverish
activity is taking place to meet the complex needs of native communities
whose right to bilingual education is now legally recognized and subsid-
ized by the state, due in no small part to the untiring efforts of people
like Mike Krauss at the University of Alaska.

Hale's specific proposals, which he placed within the context of the
Navajo language area, can be interpreted to represent the core of a
substantive general language curriculum, whose implementation has
every chance of becoming a reality in a number of communities. He has
made a convincing argument for the relevance of the application of
theoretical linguistic principles in primary and secondary language education, not only in Native American communities, but in any community.
Here also is a genuine opportunity to develop language pedagogy which
takes into account the reality of linguistic diversity. The notions of
generalization and discovery which are built into Hale's proposal should
provide the proper context for the recognition of linguistic variation and,
furthermore, should allow the identification of the factors responsible
for the variation. To illustrate with a topic which Hale himself singled
out, I would like to say a couple of words about the subject-object inversion phenomenon of Navajo. The inversion rule and the concomitant
replacement of a prefix *yi-* by a prefix *bi-* on the verb is a syntactic operation the details of which are easy to state. The conditions under which
this rule is allowed to operate, however, are governed by a semantic
hierarchy ranking the subject and object of the sentence in such a way
that the higher ranked noun must appear first. The details have been
nicely described by Mary Ellen Creamer, herself a native speaker of
Navajo (Creamer 1974). The topic has also been discussed by Hale (1973)
and by Frishberg (1972). What is not yet known about this is how much
tolerance there can be among speakers of Navajo for sentences deviating
from the hierarchy. In addition to the usual breakdown of intuitions
in the less clear cases, my own admittedly limited exposure to the speech
of two individuals reveals that for one of them the hierarchy is adhered
to quite rigidly, while for the other a much more permissive attitude
prevails. It would be possible within a program such as Hale describes to
discover the extent of such differences, their correlation with geographic-
ally defined dialects, other sociolinguistic parameters including the
amount of acculturation of the family or peer group, or simply personal
attitude. In addition, it is of considerable interest to ascertain the age
at which the hierarchy becomes part of the competence of children who
speak Navajo. In other words, at which stage of his development does

the Navajo-speaking child have sufficient control of all the variables to allow him to determine that it is perfectly appropriate in Navajo to say the equivalent of 'The boy was bitten by the dog' but not 'The dog bit the boy'. Indeed, such findings could in turn influence the manner in which this topic is handled in the classroom. It should be obvious that Navajo linguists working within their own community will make a unique contribution to both linguistic theory and educational practice. The programs they develop merit close attention as they will surely serve as models for other areas.

To take another point of view, and because my own involvement has been with communities in Southern California where the vitality of the native languages has been further eroded and the size of the communities is very small, I would like to raise the question of the relevance of linguistics to these communities, since it is a sad fact that they are more common than those where the language flourishes among a large group of people. A great need to have language questions taken seriously and handled competently exists in all these communities and the overt recognition of this need is an all-pervasive though recent phenomenon, perhaps all the more intense in those communities where awareness of language loss is now having a strong impact. When the magnitude of the problems involved is considered, it is truly remarkable that practical steps are actually being taken and individuals identified who possess the needed skills to meet these needs. It is also significant that the spontaneous decision in all cases has been the establishment of 'language classes', led by a 'teacher' who is remunerated for his efforts. The important principle being implemented in this fashion is that the skills which qualify someone as a teacher of his language are valued and worthy of financial remuneration, thus granting the teacher the status which no volunteer unpaid work can bestow. Of the same order is the desire in all cases to have the instruction take the form of a 'class', thus granting the whole enterprise an official status which a simple community gathering could not achieve. Support has come from various sources. In two cases, the Cupeño and Northern Diegueño language classes, they are part of a program of evening instruction sponsored by Palomar Community College, which is developing a Native American Studies program through which the local communities can and do make their needs known. For example, on the Pala Reservation, not only are Cupeño language classes being conducted, but, at the request of the community a large class on North American Ethnology is physically held on the reservation accompanied on the occasion I witnessed by a visit to the

new cultural center where material culture items and historical documents and photographs relevant to Cupeño history are exhibited. The
remuneration of the native language teachers by Palomar College is the
same as that for any other course taught under this program. For the
Cupeño language, Mrs. Rosinda Nolasquez, for all practical purposes the
last fluent speaker of the language, now well into her eighties, conducts
two classes with the assistance of linguists from UCSD, one for children
and one for adults, in her determination to pass on her knowledge
against all odds. On a recent occasion I had to visit the adult class, I
was impressed by the genuine interest which members of the group
obviously have in the topic, an interest which they have been able to
sustain for some time, as was dramatically demonstrated by the presence
of an extremely well-worn copy of the recent volume on the Cupeño
language by Rosinda Nolasquez and Jane Hill (Nolasquez and Hill
1973). For the Northern Diegueño class, Mr. Ted Couro, now 85, and
afflicted with poor vision and hearing, has nevertheless for the past
six years conducted some of the most imaginative classes I have ever witnessed. His cousin, Mrs. Christina Hutcheson, was a constant visitor to
his classes until shortly before her death in 1973. The sharpness of her insights were matched only by her interest in the enterprise. At age 90, she
learned to read and write her language and was able as a result to completely proofread the final version of the Dictionary of Mesa Grande
Diegueño which she co-authored with Ted Couro (Couro and Hutcheson 1973), catching inconsistencies and mistakes in both languages.
A pedagogical grammar based on Ted Couro's language classes is now
in press (Couro and Langdon in press). Royalties on the sale of these
books, which are published by the Malki Museum Press, an Indian-
owned enterprise, also accrue to the native authors. Support for other
classes, such as the Diegueño classes on the Barona Reservation and those
held at the Kumeyaay Tribal Affairs Office, has come from the BIA
and other supporting agencies. Members of the classes assiduously
volunteer to type and duplicate class materials, copies of which are
avidly collected by all concerned.

What I have witnessed in these classes is the emergence not only of a
group of dedicated teachers (who in most instances are too advanced in
age to contemplate a long career) but also the identification of a few
gifted individuals who have a good passive command of their language
and are developing literacy skills and insights into the structure of their
language as a result of attending these classes. I propose that in communities of this type, these individuals can play an important role.

Given some training in linguistic concepts and methodology, they could conduct important tasks of a linguistic nature. For example, they could undertake serious sociolinguistic investigations of their communities in an effort to determine accurately the linguistic competence of its membership, a task which no outsider can hope to properly perform. It is a well-known fact that accurate sociolinguistic data are all but lacking for American Indian communities. In fact, the best work in this area also most emphatically recognizes this deficiency. A recent fine survey of Athabaskan bilingualism (Kari and Spolsky 1974) repeatedly stresses the lack of accurate information and the elegant survey article on the "Ethnography of Speaking" just completed by Wick Miller (forthcoming) must constantly qualify its statements with the extent of our ignorance. Even some of the most basic facts, such as the number of fluent speakers, are veiled in approximations. For example, I cannot guess with any degree of accuracy the number of present speakers of Diegueño, and this in spite of my association with the community over the past ten years. And yet, it should be evident that no serious program of language teaching or development can be proposed or undertaken without a solid basic knowledge of the sociolinguistic reality to be dealt with. This does not involve only matters of degree of knowledge of the language (although this is of course of considerable importance) but also more subtle questions of attitudes toward language, and the interpretation of value judgments. For example, I often hear people comment on someone's speech, judging how well that person speaks his language. I am sometimes puzzled by these statements which more often than not do not coincide with my evaluation of the individual's competence, since these judgments can allude to such features as the use of loan words by otherwise completely fluent speakers.

In the Diegueño language area there is a great need for dialect dictionaries, since the language is spoken in several rather divergent varieties. This is another task that could be undertaken by linguistically trained members of the community with a passive command of the language. This topic is of great interest to members of the community who are always willing to discuss it at length. Such natural predilections of a group should be used to advantage in the conception of language programs and the content of pedagogical materials. No dialect is the privileged or prestige one and the notion of promoting one at the expense of the other would certainly meet strong resistance. It is more likely that each local group will adapt and develop materials to fit its own dialect, and will in the process gain a better understanding of the amount and kind of diversity found in its language. Once such individuals are identified and their interest ascertained, I believe that providing the appropriate training would not be a serious problem if the available resources of the area are brought to bear on the question. The problem of support is more complex, but the results achieved so far are encouraging enough to suggest that where there is interest and genuine talent, sources of support can usually be found.

Finally, as yet another approach to the long-term language needs of Native American communities, I would like to mention a concept which is being developed in the San Diego area, centering on the Native American Studies program at California State University at San Diego, which, under the able direction of Professor John Rouillard, is seriously committed to the notion that native languages are a crucial component of a Native American Studies Program. Among the Native American students in this program a remarkably high percentage are fluent speakers of their native language. The premise is that any student in this program has the right to expect his college education to include the acquisition of deeper insights into the structure of his language, as well as the acquisition of such skills as will enable him to pass on that knowledge to others. In addition to the regular language courses I have already mentioned, it is proposed to develop a program of language internship in collaboration with the research facilities of the UCSD Linguistics Department and Center for Research in Language Acquisition on the one hand, and the California State University Linguistics Department and teacher training program on the other. The aim is to train speakers of Native American languages in basic linguistic theory and methodology, as well as in an approach to language teaching that will enable them to conduct instruction in their own language in a variety of teaching situations. An integral part of this training will be the production of sophisticated nontechnical descriptive materials as well as the production of pedagogical materials at a variety of levels. The intent is to learn by doing within the context of a team made up of a native speaker, a linguist, and others as appropriate. Not only will this take full advantage of and develop the very special skills which these students bring with them, but the results will provide the necessary input for the training of others after them, including in particular those who have less native competence or even none at all. With the availability of appropriate materials and trained personnel to use them, some language competence can be taught at any level. After all, the basic model of western education is or at least was based solidly on the study of the Classics, and placed great emphasis on the languages of the cultures from which contemporary ones emerged. If this is at all justified in the western curriculum – and there seems to be at present a revival of interest in Latin and Greek on the part of college students – surely Native American communities have a right to access to the language of their cultural heritage, even in the extreme case where it is no longer spoken in their midst.

I am personally convinced that there is a vast untapped store of talent that can be brought to bear on these questions. My experience is that native speakers of American Indian languages tend to have a great deal of insight into language and to respond to linguistic concepts with ease. The sheer intellectual excitement of discovering interesting patterns and subtle distinctions within a body of knowledge previously taken for granted is an addictive experience and the basic fact of bilingualism and often multilingualism predisposes an individual to a receptivity to linguistic conceptualization. As one illustration among many, I would like to tell you about Cynthia Wilson, a native speaker of Kwtsaan (better known as Yuma), now completing her teacher training at California State University at San Diego, who has just started working on the syntactic structure of her language with linguists at UCSD. In an attempt to clarify the use of the predicates normally translated 'be' and 'do', she volunteered the generalization that 'be' is appropriate for 'actions', and 'do' for 'tasks'. An attempt on my part to translate this into some standard grammatical or semantic category revealed that the distinction is not transitive/intransitive, neither is it active/stative, although these notions capture some aspects of the problem; it is indeed 'action' vs. 'task', where action covers such things as singing and dancing (both transitive in Kwtsaan as well as obviously active), and task such things as making supper, building houses, etc. I propose that it would be tragic to let such talent remain untutored.

University of California, San Diego

REFERENCES

Couro, T., and C. Hutcheson. 1973. Dictionary of Mesa Grande Diegueño. Malki Museum Press.
Couro, T., and M. Langdon. 1975. Let's talk 'Iipay Aa: An introduction to Mesa Grande Diegueño. Malki Museum Press.
Creamer, M. E. 1974. Ranking in Navajo nouns. Navajo Language Review 1.29-38.
Frishberg, N. 1972. Navaho object markers and the great chain of being. Syntax and semantics, ed. by J. P. Kimball, 1.259-66. Seminar Press.

Hale, K. 1969. American Indians in linguistics: A plan and a program. The Indian Historian 2.15-18, 28.
—. 1973. A note on subject-object inversion in Navajo. Issues in linguistics. Papers in honor of Henry and Renée Kahane, 300-09. University of Illinois Press.
Kari, J., and B. Spolsky. 1974. Athapaskan language maintenance and bilingualism. Southwest Areal Linguistics 35-64. Institute for Cultural Pluralism, San Diego State University.
Miller, W. R. forthcoming. Ethnography of speaking. Handbook of North American Indians 15.
Nolasquez, R., and J. H. Hill, eds. 1973. Mulu'wetam: The first people. Cupeño Oral History and Language. Malki Museum Press.

BOAS, SAPIR, AND BLOOMFIELD

MARY R. HAAS

Franz Boas (1858-1942), Edward Sapir(1884-1939), and Leonard Bloomfield (1887-1949), taken together, dominated the field of American Indian linguistics for nearly half a century. Boas was the first and was the teacher of Edward Sapir. Leonard Bloomfield came into the field from a different route, but was also influenced by Boas through personal contact. If one recalls that American Indian languages had been studied in one fashion or another for nearly four centuries before Boas began his work, it is difficult to see at first why his impact was so great and why, indeed, many people seem to think that almost nothing was done before Boas. The difference was in approach and in the insistence on field work. Boas was trained as a physicist,[1] but he also had strong influences from the field of geography and he began his work among Eskimos and Indians in connection with that interest. Boas had his own unique way of doing field work. This consisted of writing out voluminous texts and then proceeding to translate and analyze them word by word and sentence by sentence in so far as possible.[2] When Boas began his work among the Northwest Coast Indians, almost all of them were still monolingual, or at least spoke no European language. The lingua franca of the area was the Chinook jargon and for this reason Boas learned to speak that.[3]

It must not be overlooked that linguistics was only one of the fields that Boas was interested in. More than anyone else he was a master of all fields of anthropology, and in his studies of the American Indian he was as interested in physical anthropology, archaeology, mythology, and ethnology, as in linguistics.[4] When one recalls this it is even harder to understand how he managed to accumulate such a large body of material of a linguistic nature. However, he believed that the culture could be understood through the language and not otherwise and, since so many Indians were unable to express themselves in any language other than their own, he was forced to acquire his material through the language.

As is well known, Boas's most important theoretical contribution to the study of linguistics was his promulgation of the concept of linguistic relativism, that is, that each language had to be studied in and for itself. It was not to be forced into a mold that was more appropriate to some other language. Side by side with this was his insistence on seeing the language as a whole. He was not concerned merely with phonetics, or merely with morphology, or merely with lexicography. Instead he placed equal ephasis on all of these facets. He set forth these ideas clearly and concisely in his "Introduction" to Part I of the *Handbook of American Indian Languages*, of which he was editor (Boas 1911). This Introduction became the leading statement of linguistic principles and methodology for decades to follow. Indeed it is still a most important piece of work to read. Here he set forth the various ways in which languages could differ from each other. Previously the emphasis had been on taking the categories of some familiar language and then showing how these were expressed in the language under study.[5] In addition, Boas's Introduction set forth a program of what was to be accomplished in the way of providing grammars for the languages of North America. He listed the families and language isolates that he felt should be included in his *Handbook*. Many of these grammars did appear. There were Parts 1 (1911) and 2 (1922) and finally 3 (1933-38), and then a single grammar comprised the beginning of Part 4 (1941), which was never completed. It was an ambitious program, one that perhaps could never have been completed in the form in which he envisaged it. Nevertheless it set the wheels in motion, and the work that has followed in a steady stream ever since then owes more than can possibly be expressed to Boas's penetrating vision.

As one goes through the *Handbook* today one is likely to find some of the early grammars difficult to read. The degree of sophistication that has been arrived at at present is of course the direct beneficiary of these early struggles. The early pieces have strange phonetic symbols and long and difficult descriptions of many features that can be handled today with considerably more ease. Still if these pioneering grammars had not been written we certainly would not be able to do what we can do today.

Although Boas from time to time mentioned that certain languages might be related to one another, he was not primarily interested in the field of linguistic classification. I think he recognized that Powell's 1891 classification was adequate for general purposes,[6] and only now and then did he venture any suggestions beyond that. He was early intrigued by structural similarities between Tlingit and Haida and the Athapaskan languages, a subject which even today is controversial. Moreover, in his later years he felt that attempts to place such difficult languages in a larger schema was an idle exercise. Later this became something of a bone of contention between Boas on the one hand and Sapir and Kroeber on the other.

Edward Sapir was the student of Franz Boas. Boas dominated the whole field of American anthropology for half a century and, with his strong personality, he also dominated those who studied under him. No one dared to cross him in any significant way and they all looked for the master's approval. Of course there is no question but that Sapir would have been a great scholar even if he had never met Boas, but the direction of his talents would have been other than it was. Although he was already something of a Germanic scholar at the time he met Boas, Boas made him feel that he still had everything to learn about language.

Sapir had a very keen ear and was able to record the difficult languages of the West with great facility. He espoused the relativistic and holistic approaches of Boas. He recorded and analyzed a voluminous amount of material on Takelma, a language of Oregon which has since passed into oblivion. As his doctoral dissertation, he prepared a lengthy grammar of Takelma (Sapir 1912) which Boas published in Part 2 of the *Handbook*; he also published texts and a vocabulary (Sapir 1909). In his concluding section of the grammar he presents a sort of thumb-nail sketch of the language, contrasting it with some of the neighboring languages and enumerating some of its more 'typical American' traits (Sapir 1912:282):

Some of the more important of these typical or at any rate widespread American traits, that are found in Takelma, are: the incorporation of the pronominal (and nominal) object in the verb; the incorporation of the possessive pronouns in the noun; the closer association with the verb-form of the object than the subject; the inclusion of a considerable number of instrumental and local modifications in the verb-complex; the weak development of differences of tense in the verb and of number in the verb and noun; and the impossibility of drawing a sharp line between mode and tense.

He clearly savored every nuance of every language that he worked on and the wonder of it all is that he worked on so many. As an aside, at this point it is of interest to point out that Sapir frequently required students in his seminar to prepare a thumb-nail sketch of each of the languages we had been analyzing. Such a sketch had to be written by making only the most minimal use of actual linguistic forms.[7]

Sapir spent fifteen years in Ottawa, where he became Chief Ethnologist

in the Division of Anthropology, Geological Survey, of the Canadian
National Museum. He had the occasion to do considerable field work –
it was at this time that he undertook his lengthy work on the Nootka
language. In addition he turned his attention very seriously to working
out a revised classification of the American Indian languages north of
Mexico. The standard classification was Powell's, which set up fifty-five
linguistic families north of Mexico. The area of California alone had
twenty-two. Sapir had previously started some work on the California
languages, particularly on Yana, which he carried out during a year
spent here. He became familiar with the work of Dixon and Kroeber
who were trying to reduce the twenty-two families to a smaller number.
Sapir was interested in their efforts and also made his own contributions
to them. It may have been this that set him to thinking about the continent
as a whole. He eventually compressed the fifty-five Powellian families into
six superstocks. This involved him in a variety of classificatory and comparative endeavors. He carried out comparative linguistic studies within
certain families, for example Uto-Aztecan and Athapaskan, and published
important contributions to both of these. But when it came to putting
larger groups together, this could not be carried out with the same kind
of rigorous comparison but entailed making use of other kinds of devices,
including rather specific types of structural and morphological similarities. Perhaps the grandest scheme that Sapir came up with was the
Hokan-Siouan, which included many of the languages of California,
of Texas, and of the Northeast and Southeast as well as some of Mexico
and Central America. The typological characteristics that he assigns
to the superstock are stated by him to be:

The Hokan-Siouan languages are prevailingly agglutinative, tend to use
prefixes rather than suffixes for the more formal elements, particularly
the pronominal elements of the verbs; distinguish active and static verbs; and
make free use of compounding of stems and of nominal incorporation. (Sapir
1929).

His ultimate classification into six superstocks finally appeared in the
Encyclopaedia Britannica of 1929. By that time he was teaching at the
University of Chicago and was soon to go to Yale. At Yale his interests
moved on in other directions and he seems not to have cared too much
about continuing his classificatory activities, at least not in North
America. However, several of his students became interested and were
inspired by his work to carry on similar activities later on in their lives.

As was hinted earlier, Sapir's ambitious projects in regard to the
classification of American Indian languages were not viewed with

approval by Boas. One of the controversies that ensued arose from Sapir's attempt to set up a superstock, Nadené, consisting of the Athapaskan languages plus Tlingit and Haida. Pliny Earle Goddard, a former missionary who had studied Hupa and a number of other Athapaskan languages, did not accept this relationship and published an article refuting Sapir's claims. Boas concurred in Goddard's position. This particular problem is still not completely amenable to solution. While there are strong structural similarities between Tlingit and Haida and the Athapaskan languages, the kind of cognates that one would like to find to clinch the matter are not easy to come by and so the matter remains controversial to this day. Perhaps the most remarkable of Sapir's discoveries about distant or previously unsuspected relationships was the case of the connection that he postulated between the Algonkian family of languages and Yurok and Wiyot, small language communities of northwestern California. The latter two languages had been placed together by Dixon and Kroeber, since they displayed certain similarities, but no one had previously dreamed that they could possibly be related to the Algonkian family of languages lying far to the East. When Sapir set forth his evidence he was attacked by Truman Michelson, the leading Algonkianist of the time. And Boas concurred in Michelson's position. Sapir never lost his belief in this particular relationship, but since it had been a matter of such severe controversy it was not generally accepted. Even European scholars, such as C. C. Uhlenbeck, viewed it with skepticism. As it turns out, this was probably one of the best of Sapir's amalgamations and today there is general agreement with Sapir's position that Algonkian, Yurok, and Wiyot are indeed genetically related (Haas 1958). Many of the far-reaching schemes that he set up other than this, however, still open up enormous vistas for future work and will not be solved for a long time to come.

Sapir was not only an inspiring teacher, he was also an unusually gifted writer who also tried his hand at poetry. His linguistic and cultural papers are often gems of exposition and can be read for their style with as much pleasure as for their content. Among other activities of the Ottawa period was the production of a general book called *Language* (Sapir 1921), which still remains a classic.

Bloomfield entered the field of American Indian languages not through training in anthropology but from another direction, namely the study of foreign languages and Germanic and Indo-European philology.[8] Nevertheless, Bloomfield recognized the value of culture and ethnology for the study of linguistics. Moreover, he was influenced by Boas even though he was not a student of Boas. He himself recognized his indebtedness in his obituary of Boas when he says: "He taught William Jones, Truman Michelson, Edward Sapir, and others now living, and with unfailing kindness he helped many who were not formally his pupils (Bloomfield 1943:198). I think Bloomfield included himself in the latter category. He also acclaims Boas as one who had contributed so very much to the development of descriptive language study, saying, in this same obituary: "The native languages of our country had been studied by some very gifted men, but none had succeeded in putting this study upon a scientific basis. The scientific equipment of linguists, on the other hand, contained few keen tools except the comparative method and this could not yet be here applied." I suspect he also appreciated Boas because of the latter's insistence on a large body of textual material.

Bloomfield's thoughts about doing field work are expressed in a review of one of Michelson's works (Bloomfield 1922:276):

One can imagine few more fascinating experiences in the study of mankind than to hear an Algonquian language spoken and to appreciate upon closer study the marvellous complexity of what one has heard. The scientific problem is correspondingly difficult. I believe that the solution, short of giving linguistic training to a native speaker, lies in the way of *sich einleben* – the notation of everyday speech and the attempt to become, to whatever extent is possible, a member of the speech-community.

Bloomfield's most important contributions to the study of American Indian languages are, first, his descriptive studies of Fox (on the basis of William Jones's work) and Cree, Menomini, and Ojibwa (on the basis of his own field work), and secondly, his very careful comparative studies of these four languages. He insisted that the descriptive studies had to precede the comparative studies and he set out to provide an outstanding example of this principle. When he undertook his comparative work on these languages, he was motivated by a strong desire to refute the idea, common among European linguists, that unwritten languages did not lend themselves to the kind of rigorous comparative study that could be applied to written languages. His admirable article "On the Sound System of Central Algonquian" (1925) successfully refuted this notion, and in a footnote to the article he makes it clear that this was an important reason for preparing it. He says (Bloomfield 1925:130):

I hope, also, to help dispose of the notion that the usual processes of linguistic change are suspended on the American continent (Meillet and Cohen, *Les langues du monde*, Paris 1924, p. 9). If there exists anywhere a language in which these processes do not occur (sound-change independent of meaning, analogic change, etc.), then they will not explain the history of Indo-European or of any other language. A principle such as the regularity of phonetic change is not part of the specific tradition handed on to each new speaker of a given language, but is either a universal trait of human speech or nothing at all, an error.

Later, in his "Algonquian" sketch (1946), he provided a fuller exposition of the character of Proto Algonkian, including morphology as well as phonology.

Unlike Sapir, Bloomfield had no interest in deeper comparative studies and so he did not enter into any of the controversies in this area. In his Algonkian sketch he mentions that Wiyot and Yurok are alleged to be related to Algonkian, but he himself does not make any commitment on this score. I suspect he felt that such studies would be premature, that one needed to progress step by step and amass all the necessary material on Proto-Algonkian before proceeding to make deeper studies.

In 1914 Bloomfield published a book called *An Introduction to the Study of Language* and this was a great improvement on anything that was then available on general language study. It is interesting that one of the reviewers complains that he quotes too often from unusual or lesser known languages, among which the reviewer includes Russian! In 1933 Bloomfield published a book called *Language* which was a complete revision, indeed a new writing, of his earlier book. This book became the basis of a school of linguistics which later came to be known as 'structural linguistics'. Bloomfield himself seems to have used the word 'descriptive linguistics', or sometimes 'synchronic linguistics' (Saussure's term), for a careful study of any individual language without regard to its history and further, of course, to distinguish this from contrastive and comparative linguistics.

Through this book Bloomfield became a leader in the field of general linguistics quite apart from his important contributions to the study of American Indian languages. At the same time, because of this book and also because of the general works of Boas and Sapir, the field of American Indian languages began to have an impact upon general linguistic studies that it had not previously had. Consequently, it can be said that the study of American Indian languages had an impact on American linguistic theory in the first half of this century which was almost as great as that which the study of Indo-European and classical languages had had in the nineteenth century. The work of Boas, Sapir, and Bloomfield on languages that previously had not been written down by anyone opened up a whole new era of linguistic study. Techniques of field methods had to be developed, phonetic systems had to be developed, and this very struggle with ways to write down previously unwritten languages led to the development of the American version of classical phonemic theory. Certainly this whole notion would never have emerged as a problem if linguists had continued to work only on written languages. American Indian languages opened up other vistas as well. These included the possibility of testing the applicability of the comparative method to unwritten languages. Both Bloomfield and Sapir rose to this challenge and Sapir presented some of their results in a fascinating article entitled "The Concept of Phonetic Law as Tested in Primitive Languages by Leonard Bloomfield" (1931) in which he presented results obtained by Bloomfield in respect to Algonkian and by himself in respect to Athapaskan.

Other problems did not receive equal attention among the three great minds. Sapir in particular was interested in what should properly be called classificatory linguistics, because while ideally it should rest on comparative linguistics, practically it often does not. Neither Boas nor Bloomfield were interested in building up larger groupings of languages of the type proposed by Sapir. Unlike Sapir and Bloomfield, Boas did not make any significant contributions to comparative linguistics, although he set out some of the sound correspondences of the Salishan languages in collaboration with his student Haeberlin. But the one thing that Boas emphasized more than anyone else was what has more recently come to be known as areal linguistics. Perhaps it was his early interest in geography that led him in this direction. He was interested in the distribution of traits in mythology, in culture and in languages. He returned to this problem again and again, and his position was for the most part not properly understood by Sapir or by Kroeber, who felt that he was using this as a weapon against their classificatory schemes. Kroeber even accused Boas of being 'antihistorical' in his attitude. This puzzled Boas because, as he saw it, these interests were as validly historical as were classificatory interests. He even went so far as to say (Boas 1920:375):

If these observations regarding the influence of acculturation upon language should be correct, then the whole history of American languages must not be treated on the assumption that all languages which show similarities must be considered as branches of the same linguistic family. ... In other words, the whole theory of an Ursprache for every group of modern languages must be held in abeyance until we can prove that these languages go back to a single stock and that they have not originated, to a large extent, by the process of acculturation.

Boas's position in turn both puzzled and infuriated people like Sapir and Kroeber, who wished to make genetic classifications of these languages in so far as they possibly could. I think it's fair to say that today there is much more sympathy and understanding for Boas's point of view than there was in the past. His programmatic statement of 1920 can be readily accepted today because we no longer view it as opposition to genetic classification (Boas 1920:376):

Firstly, we must study the differentiation of dialects like those of the Siouan, Muskhogean, Algonquian, Shoshonean, Salishan, and Athapascan. Secondly, we must make a detailed study of the distribution of phonetic, grammatical, and lexicographical phenomena, the latter including also particularly the principles upon which the grouping of concepts is based [e.g. shape, as in classificatory verbs]. Finally, our study ought to be directed not only to an investigation of the similarities of the languages, but equally intensively toward their dissimilarities. *Only on this basis can we hope to solve the general historical problem.* [Emphasis added.]

But I should not leave the impression that Sapir was unaware of or uninterested in borrowings and diffusion and the like. He saw their significance too, and in part he needed some of his larger groupings in order to highlight the differences between what he considered to be genetic and what might be considered diffused. He gives some examples of this in his famous paper on "Time Perspective" (1916), where he finds that certain traits, such as the use of instrumental verb prefixes, appear both in Maidu and in nearby Washo and Shasta-Achomawi (also Shoshonean), and he is interested in the fact that on the basis of the Dixon and Kroeber classification Maidu belongs to Penutian, while the neighboring Washo and Shasta-Achomawi are Hokan.

In summing up, I should say that Boas will be remembered for his editing of the *Handbook of American Indian Languages,* for the founding of the *International Journal of American Linguistics,* for his work on Kwakiutl, Dakota, and many other languages, and for his insistence on the study of areal phenomena. (Boas was also probably the first to train American Indians as linguists.)[9] Sapir will be remembered for his seminal work on Uto-Aztecan, Athapaskan, and Hokan-Coahuiltecan, for his grand classificatory schemes which we are still in the process of testing, for his meticulous grammars of Takelma, Southern Paiute, and other languages, and also for his book *Language.* Bloomfield in turn will be remembered for his work on Proto Algonkian, in which he demonstrated the way in which unwritten languages can be reconstructed both as to their phonology and their morphology, for his synchronic studies of Fox, Cree, Menomini, and Ojibwa, and of course for his influential book *Language*.

In his poignant dedication for *Linguistic Structures of Native America* Bloomfield spoke of Boas as "the teacher, in one or another sense, of us all" (Hoijer et al. 1946:5). Here it is fitting to make the same statement in regard to all three of these great men as the teachers, in one or another sense, of all who are working in the field today.

University of California, Berkeley

REFERENCES

Bloomfield, L. 1909-10. A semasiological differentiation in Germanic Ablaut. Modern Philology 7.245-382.
—. 1914. An introduction to the study of language. New York: Henry Holt and Company/London: G. Bell.
—. 1922. Review of The Owl Sacred Pack of the Fox Indians by T. Michelson. American Journal of Philology 43.276-81.
—. 1925. On the sound System of Central Algonquian. Language 1.130-56.
—. 1933. Language. New York: Henry Holt and Company.
—. 1943. [Obituary of Boas]. Language 19.198.
—. 1946. Algonquian. Linguistic structures of Native America, by H. Hoijer et al., 85-129. New York: Viking Fund Publications in Anthropology 6.
Boas, F. ed. 1911. Handbook of American Indian languages Part 1. Bureau of American Ethnology Bulletin 40. Washington D.C. "Introduction" reprinted by Georgetown University Press, n.d.
—. 1920. The classification of American Indian languages. American Anthropologist 22.367-76. Reprinted in Boas 1940:211-18.
—. ed. 1922. Handbook of American Indian languages Part 2. Bureau of American Ethnology Bulletin 40. Washington D.C.
—. ed. 1933-38. Handbook of American Indian languages Part 3. Columbia University Press. (J. J. Augustin: Glückstadt-Hamburg-New York.)
—. 1940. Race, language, and culture. New York: Macmillan.
—, ed. 1941. Handbook of American Indian languages Part 4. New York: J. J Augustin.
Haas, M. R. 1958. Algonkian-Ritwan: The end of a controversy. International Journal of American Linguistics 24.159-73.
Hoijer, H. et al., 1946. Linguistic structures of Native America. New York: Viking Fund Publications in Anthropology 6.
Powell, J. W. 1891. Linguistic families of North America North of Mexico. Washington D.C.: Bureau of [American] Ethnology Annual Report 7 (1885-86).
Sapir, E. 1909. Takelma texts. University of Pennsylvania, Anthropological Publications 2:1.1-263.

—. 1912. The Takelma language of Southwestern Oregon. First issued as an extract from the Handbook of American Indian languages Part 2, ed. by F. Boas. Washington D.C.: Bureau of American Ethnology Bulletin 40.

—. 1916. Time perspective in aboriginal American culture: A study in method. Canada, Department of Mines, Geological Survey Memoir 90, Anthropological Series no. 13. Ottawa: Government Printing Bureau. Reprinted in Selected Writings of Edward Sapir, ed. by D. G. Mandelbaum, 389-467. Berkeley and Los Angeles: University of California Press 1949.

—. 1921. Language: An introduction to the study of speech. New York: Harcourt, Brace.

—. 1929. Central and North American languages. Encyclopaedia Britannica 14th edition 5.138-41. Reprinted in Selected Writings of Edward Sapir, ed. by D. G. Mandelbaum, 169-78. Berkeley and Los Angeles: University of California Press 1949.

—. 1931. The concept of phonetic law as tested in primitive languages by Leonard Bloomfield. Methods in Social Science: A Case Book, ed. by S. A. Rice, 297-306. Reprinted in Selected Writings of Edward Sapir, ed. by D. G. Mandelbaum 73-82. Berkeley and Los Angeles: University of California Press, 1949.

NOTES

[1] He received the Ph. D. at the University of Kiel in 1881. His dissertation was *Contributions to the understanding of the color of sea water.*

[2] He also relied on native speakers to write out texts for him, both materials of their own and materials from other Indians. Among the Kwakiutl, George Hunt furnished texts to Boas for over forty years.

[3] One cannot help but wonder how adequate the jargon was to translate the many texts he was obtaining. However, he appears to have relied on his own ability to fill in those things that were not adequately expressed in the jargon.

[4] None who followed him ever achieved his stature in all of these fields. However, he expected his students to learn something of all of them. Many of them rebelled. Sapir, for example, refused to take up physical anthropology.

[5] This approach resulted in such ridiculous statements as "This language has no gender. In order to indicate gender it is necessary to add the word 'man' to indicate the masculine and 'woman' to indicate the feminine." Unfortunately this kind of nonsense was not uncommon and usually resulted in overlooking the actually existing categories of the particular language.

[6] However, he was aware of its limitations: "Much of the material on which Major Powell's work is based is exceedingly scanty, and it is obvious that more accurate studies will show relationships which at the time could not be safely inferred" (Boas 1920).

[7] The above quotation is only a part of such a thumb-nail of Takelma.

[8] See his doctoral dissertation on Germanic Secondary Ablaut (Bloomfield 1909-10).

[9] Prominent among American Indians whom he trained as linguists were William Jones, a Fox Indian, and Ella Deloria, a Dakota Sioux. See also footnote 2.

BOAS, SAPIR, AND BLOOMFIELD

DISCUSSION BY DAVID S. ROOD

I feel very much the way Margaret Langdon claimed to feel yesterday, namely that all the points I wanted to make have already been made. Nevertheless, I can mention a few special perspectives on the things we have been talking about which the study of Boas, Sapir, and Bloomfield may give us. For one thing, it is worth noting that a number of the suggestions presented yesterday were already part of the plans and ideas of one or more of these three pioneers. For example, as Haas mentioned briefly, Boas did indeed train American Indians to be linguists, at least as he conceived of the profession. Perhaps the most outstanding example was Ella Deloria, and I can report from personal experience that the Boas/Deloria grammar of Dakota (1941) is a superbly complete and useful description of that language to this day. Moreover, in typical Boas/Sapir fashion, Deloria also provided us with large quantities of Dakota textual materials, which can form the basis of linguistic and folkloristic studies of many kinds. So we would seem to have fine precedent of long standing for the idea that training a native speaker as a linguist can greatly benefit the field.

A second point made yesterday was that American languages may serve as a laboratory for general linguistic studies. Of course this has always been accepted procedure in North America, but now that linguistic theory is focusing more and more on universal properties of language it is imperative that the utilization of this laboratory increase. Papers testing the proposals of theoretical linguistics (usually derived from English data) on Amerindian languages are becoming more and more frequent, though disappointingly often they go unpublished or are published in relatively obscure places where they are seen only by other Americanists.[1] The reverse situation, the evolution of theories by Americanists, is today far less common, however. About the only recent theory of language to be formulated by a linguist knowledgeable in Amerindian structures is Chafe's (Chafe 1970a, b in particular) and much of the depth and coherence of that particular theory is directly attributable to the author's acquaintance with American structures.

To turn now specifically to the Boas, Sapir, Bloomfield trio, I should first like to underline two of the points Haas has made. First, I think it is difficult to overemphasize both the importance and the current relevance of Boas' Introduction to the Handbook (1911). It is astonishing how many of the points made there are the same as those one must make when teaching beginning linguistics students today. Certainly one thing American linguistics has not done in the last 50-75 years is to educate the general public very much about language or languages. In this connection, I was intrigued yesterday by Hale's proposals for teaching linguistics in the Navajo elementary school, and would like to see similar kinds of activities evolved for monolingual English speaking children.

The second point in Haas's paper which I should like to emphasize is the statement to the effect that Indian languages and the linguists' field problems to some extent dictated the form of American linguistic theory. Often overlooked in the polemics which were so frequent around 15 years ago against taxonomic phonology and immediate constituent syntax were the facts which these theories were evolved to explain and describe. Without mechanical recording devices, only the very gifted like Boas or Sapir themselves could do much accurate text transcription – and if you don't believe that, look at the Dorsey/Swanton Biloxi texts, or recall the amount of linguistic material that has never left the collector's field notes because that collector is reluctant to let people see his inconsistent recordings. A biunique taxonomic phonemic analysis, arrived at by relatively mechanical discovery procedures, gives a recorder a quick and easy way to write down dictated material. It seems only natural that such a useful field tool should rapidly achieve the status of a theoretically important device.

As for syntax, again the field work situation and the tasks the masters set for themselves and their students unavoidably forced linguistic theory to concern itself with analysis rather than synthesis. One had to segment forms and classify morphemes to comprehend the texts being recorded and thus get at the information they contained. Although all three of these men learned to speak some of their field languages,[2] none of them ever evolved for their students a theory for generating utterances. Bloomfield, as a professional language teacher, might have been expected to present his material in such a way that the reader could learn the language from it, and as a matter of fact his grammars are easier to follow than the others', perhaps partly because of his understanding of language pedagogy.[3]

In sum, then, American linguistic theory up to the middle of this century was in large part the result of the purposes for which the grammars were written and of the data with which the theory had to cope. Boas, Sapir, and Bloomfield all evolved theories, some more coherently articulated than others, of course, but theories appropriate to their data and situations.

The final two points I would like to make concern the actual language data collection and description carried out by these scholars. The first of these is that their descriptions, contrary to the folklore of our profession, are not all that difficult to read and use. The second is that these descriptions are far too neglected both by language theoreticians and by teachers of linguistics.

With respect to the problems of reading Boas' or Sapir's earlier grammars, Haas mentioned the problem of strange phonetic symbols; but I submit that it does not really take very much study of the first few pages of any of the grammars to get a fairly good idea of what each of these symbols means. Surely linguists should be the last people in the world to admit to difficulties with strange orthographies, particularly when these are used with the tremendous consistency which is typical of all three of these pioneers.

Second, of course, is the problem of a lack of organizational principles for the grammatical descriptions. This becomes obvious most quickly when one compares the longer sketches, such as the Kwakiutl and Chinook by Boas in the Handbook, with some of his shorter papers on small parts of languages (see Boas 1892 and 1904 among many others). The longer descriptions seem confused at first, with the discussion organized by morphological process and position class and the multitude of unassembled allomorphs cropping up here and there throughout the work. There is a general unwillingness (indeed a theoretically justified conscious refusal) to abstract and present uniformity underlying superficial variation, and this makes understanding the language hard work for the reader. In contrast, the short sketches have either left out the confusing details or organized them better, and they are straightforward and easily comprehended. The terminology employed is sometimes traditional and sometimes invented for the situation; in neither case is that a problem. Most importantly, these descriptions contain a tremendous wealth of amply illustrated information about languages, and this information should not be ignored just because it takes a little work to dig out.

So I would like to add another voice to those raised yesterday, and assert not only that there is a place in the world for current and future Americanist studies, but also that we must not neglect the results of the work of the past – in particular, of the detailed, painstaking, specific language descriptions of these pioneers of our field. Let us not be put off by strange symbols. If American languages contain important data for theories of abstract linguistic structures and substantive universals (and we all know they do), let us start making use of the data in these works, and show our students and colleagues that the materials here, though strange, are valuable and useable.

University of Colorado

REFERENCES

Boas, F. 1892. Notes on the Chemakum language. American Anthropologist 5.37-44.
—. 1904. The vocabulary of the Chinook language. American Anthropologist n.s. 6.118-47.
—. 1911. Introduction. Handbook of American Indian languages Part 1. Bureau of American Ethnology, Bulletin 40. Washington D.C.
—, and E. Deloria. 1941. Dakota grammar. Memoir of the National Academy of Sciences 23, Part 2.
Chafe, W. L. 1970a. A semantically based sketch of Onondaga. International Journal of American Linguistics Memoir 25.
—. 1970b. Meaning and the structure of language. Chicago: University of Chicago Press.
Deloria, E. 1932. Dakota texts. Publications of the American Ethnological Society 14. Reprinted 1974, New York: AMS Press.
Hockett, C. F., ed. 1970. A Leonard Bloomfield anthology. Bloomington: Indiana University Press.
Kroeber, A. L., and R. H. Lowie, eds. 1959. The anthropology of Fanz Boas. American Anthropological Association Memoir 89.

NOTES

[1] Examples are the excellent collection of papers in *Linguistic Notes from La Jolla* No. 5, 1973, or the journal *Diné Bizaad Nánil'įįh* [The Navajo Language Review]. Of course journals like *IJAL* are widely read by non-Americanists, and many papers important for linguistic theory are published there. This comment is merely intended to suggest that wider circulation of more of the laboratory reports might be beneficial to linguistic theoreticians.
[2] Boas spoke at least Chinook Jargon (according to Haas) and some Kwakiutl (see Mead quoting Boas in Kroeber and Lowie 1959:43); Sapir spoke (among others) enough Yana to be able to communicate with Ishi when he was first found; and it is legendary that Bloomfield believed firmly in doing his field work with as little English as possible, often by living with monolingual families.

[3] In this context one should note Bloomfield's remark (Hockett 1970:541) to the effect that he could not 'read' a grammar, but had to excerpt and file everything before he could learn about the language. He does not say whether or not grammars should be this way.

SOME RECENT (AND NOT SO RECENT) ATTEMPTS TO INTERPRET SEMANTICS OF NATIVE LANGUAGES IN NORTH AMERICA

C. F. AND F. M. VOEGELIN

INTERIORIZED KNOWLEDGE OF SEMANTICS

The native speaker's interiorized knowledge of his language has been exploited in many ways in fieldwork, as for example, (a) in eliciting from a native speaker by an anthropological linguist who does not speak the language under investigation; (b) in training adult speakers of exotic languages in linguistics, in the hope that they can then become professionals who communicate their interiorized knowledge of their native language to others; (c) in attaining native-like fluency by a missionary or a British social anthropologist who then converses with native speakers in their own language.[1]

The central difficulty with (a) – eliciting from a native speaker – is that one can never be sure whether certain rejected sentences are rejected because they are ungrammatical or because they are culturally inappropriate. The native speaker can indeed evaluate – in terms of their acceptability or unacceptability – the constructions which are presented to him. He/she may find acceptable some sentences which are very understandable but still not grammatical. A greater difficulty remains: to interpret what the native speaker regards as unacceptable. Is it ungrammatical? Is it grammatical but not plausible as a sentence by itself, or not plausible as a sentence fantasied to be in a discourse in which it does not belong? Is it the sort of construction which would not be acceptable in one culture space but might be acceptable in another culture space in the same society?

The difficulty with (b) – training speakers of native languages to be linguists – is the lack of good academic jobs which, were they available, might provide motivation for speakers to specialize in the analysis of a language spoken by a few thousand or a few hundred or even fewer native speakers. Contrast this with the situation of professional linguists whose native language is shared by millions and is a language of higher education. The former cannot afford – in the academic world as it is now constituted – to contemplate narcissistically nothing but the image of their own language; the latter can and often do.

Finally, the central difficulty with (c) – field workers attaining native-like fluency – is that it is effectively restricted to 'rapid-language-learners' – i.e. to those who not only share the common human competence for acquiring a systematized phonology, essential grammar, and central vocabulary of their first language or languages by the end of childhood, but in addition carry over or continue this first language facility into the acquisition of second languages after childhood.

The various problems encountered in the practice of the three forms of exploitation of the native speaker's interiorized knowledge mentioned above share a common underlying difficulty, but this is scarcely ever mentioned today. What is now taken for granted was stressed by Franz Boas who was the first in this century to train professional anthropological linguists. Boas (under the influence of Freud?) was inclined to speak of grammar as being 'unconscious' knowledge. This is of course known today as the almost total unawareness by the native speaker of the rules of his grammar, which he interiorizes before the end of childhood.[2]

But Boas went beyond characterizing grammar as 'unconscious' knowledge; he contrasted this – much to Lévi-Strauss' current regret – with a different kind of non-unawareness of the same speaker of his native culture. The person-in-the-culture has a kind of awareness of his native culture – as reflected by the fact that he is ready or even anxious (without any training at all) to talk about his native culture. What he says, Boas called 'secondary rationalizations'. In other words, what the person-in-the-culture is apt to utter are stereotypes about what goes on in his own society, unreliable or even spurious. For example, contrast what the trained anthropologist, Rappaport, claims to be the function of *Pigs for the Ancestors* and the 'secondary rationalizations' that the persons-in-the-culture make about these pigs (Rappaport 1967).

This is one of the few salient differences between language and culture. Otherwise the two have been merged in the conventional wisdom of anthropology which is reflected in every beginners textbook ('language is part of culture'), and widely borrowed in related fields – most recently by an eminent linguist (Robins 1974).

If language is part of culture, why is it that the acquisition of language (to repeat: the essential rules of phonology and grammar, and the central vocabulary) is completed by the end of childhood, while the acquisition of culture begins in childhood and continues in every step of the life cycle?

Though he does not claim this, it seems to us that Hale (1973 and 1975) has hit upon the first feasible approach for really grappling with questions of this sort which are central to the old (and continuing) language and culture studies in anthropology, and to the current specializations in sociolinguistics, psycholinguistics, and symbolic interactionism. In short, what is proposed is that a person who knows the central vocabulary and the rules of phonology and grammar of his native non-English language should be led to an awareness of what he already knows without awareness (e.g. in the bilingual education of Navajo children). The teacher should take advantage of the already acquired and interiorized knowledge by teaching the children to formulate rules of grammar and innovate vocabulary in the language which they spoke before they spoke English.

The implications of this proposal are unbelievably exciting, for it suggests that man's interiorized knowledge of his native language is quite near the surface, and not buried so deeply as to require years of training by a gifted linguist before it can be mined.[3] Nor is the proposal merely programmatic; it is solidly based on Hale's work with Navajo children. A number of language games have already been given these children; the object of each game is to teach the children to formulate an appropriate rule.[4]

Thus, one game calls for a semantic generalization. The teacher says a sentence in Navajo which can be rendered in English in approximate Navajo word order as

(1)   *the blanket give me* (beedléí shaa niłtsóós).

Then the teacher replaces the word for *blanket* with the Navajo words for *paper, cloth, shirt, leather, skirt* – or other words and asks the children to volunteer a list like this, and 'to state the property which is shared by all members of the list'. Eventually, the children (some? one of them?) will hit upon the fact that the verb in (1) 'requires that its object be a noun which denotes an object which is flexible and flat ...'.

Another game is to present the children with a sentence which is ungrammatical in one respect, but practically understandable, as

(2)   **I* is-working* (*shí naalnish).

It turns out to be (in Navajo and English, and perhaps in every natural language) 'very easy to construct ungrammatical sentences to focus on almost any area of grammar'. The children, of course, can say what is ungrammatical about the sentences presented to them only by stating what rule is violated. The violation exemplified here (in sentence 2) is shared by English; that in the following example is of course language-particular for Navajo.

This is because nouns of Navajo (unlike those of English) 'are ranked; [in reference to the rule permitting passive transformation the ranking means that] the rule applies optionally where the subject and object are equal in rank, it blocks where the subject outranks the object [(3) following], and it is obligatory, where the object outranks the subject [(4) following]'. The children then (before gaining awareness of the rule which they actualize in their speech) try to state what it is that blocks certain sentences, as (3) and (4) in Navajo.

(3) *The plate is being licked by the dog* (*leets'aa' łééchąą'í biłnaad).
(4) *The bee stung the boy* (*tśis'ná ashkii yishish).

Since the passive of (3) is blocked in Navajo, the only way of saying this would be in the active:

(3b) *The dog is licking the plate*

(because the subject outranks the object).
And the only way of saying (4) in Navajo would be in the passive:

(4b) *The boy was stung by the bee*

(where the semantic object, *boy*, outranks the semantic subject, *bee*).

HISTORICAL PERSPECTIVE AND SCOPE NOTE

Attempts to solve semantic problems in North American Indian languages were numerous early in this century under the impact of Boas (1911 and 1917) and Sapir (1917 and 1929); less numerous when linguistics became more explicit, more rigorous, and more formal under the impact of Bloomfield after 1933, when most Americanists heeded Bloomfield's advice to postpone consideration of unsolved or unresolved semantic problems until the more formal problems of grammar (in phonology and syntax) were better stated.[5]

This, in turn, gave way to a kind of linguistics – in the present last third of the century – that calls for explanation (e.g. that distinguishes, for one example, between what is language-particular and what constitutes, in typological terms, a sub-system shared by many languages or by all – language universals; and for another example, that distinguishes variable rules from categorial rules (more or less in Labov's sense)).

Yet, though linguists in both the first third and last third of the century set high store on semantic expectations, their expectations turn out to be antonymous. The pre-Bloomfield linguists expected to find that American Indian languages, cut off from Old World languages by not less than ten millennia, would reveal grammatical categories and lexical domains hitherto unknown and strange to behold.[6] And now some contemporary linguists expect that the semantic bases of the New and Old World languages will look alike, when stated more or less abstractly; but Sapir had already anticipated this expectation which is subscribed to today even by linguists who are most critical of the homogeneity hypothesis, as is Labov, who nonetheless admits that "More than any other field concerned with human behavior, linguistics has succeeded in isolating the invariant structures underlying the surface phenomena ..." (1972: 252).

What is looked for in semantics certainly influences what is found. In the pre-Bloomfield period semantic diversity was looked for; but less was found than expected. Swadesh (1946) worked in the Bloomfield period when he edited and supplemented *American Indian Grammatical Categories*, written by Edward Sapir in 1929. By then Sapir's sample of Indian languages was wide enough to enable him to say that their grammatical categories were for the most part those expectable in natural languages ("... any grammatical category to be found elsewhere in the world is sure to have a near analog somewhere in the native languages of the New World")–that what was most striking was the 'variety of languages' in the New World, exceeding those of the Old World (or at least exceeding 'European forms of speech ... in phonetic elements and peculiarities of structure'). The aboriginal languages of America (without reference to their genetic classification) "now present the most bewildering diversities of form. They are at once the delight and the despair of the linguistic student." Note well that Sapir's introductory paragraphs about diversity do not even allude to semantics; but later he predicts that what the 'linguistic student' now reports will turn out to bear upon 'an eventual philosophy of speech', since what is reported about American Indian languages has 'something of that ... uncanny, subterranean relevance to the psychology of thought and of patterned expression' that mathematics has to concrete physical problems.

The diversity, in Sapir's view, is immediately apparent and approachable in 'the forms themselves' [syntax and phonology]; it is – we interpret with emphasis – *exclusively through the mediation of the forms themselves that grammatical categories can be seen and approached*: for example, if words in a language are not marked for cases, that language

is said to be 'innocent of cases'. For Sapir, and for linguists beginning
work in the Bloomfield period, the grammatical category of case was
granted for languages in some families (e.g. Penutian languages and
languages in the Uto-Aztecan family) where 'syntactic and local cases'
are marked by constituents of the word 'analogous to the cases of the
older Indo-European languages'; some other American Indian languages
'perhaps the majority of them, are as innocent of cases as modern
French'. (In Case Grammar, of course, French is by no means innocent
of 'syntactic' cases; and American Indian languages often mark several
'local cases' though only one so-called 'syntactic case' – e.g. in Hopi
object is marked and subject unmarked, but in Yavapai subject is marked
and object is unmarked.)

Besides cases, including an identification of Eskimo ergativity (though
without using the term 'ergative'), other grammatical categories are
sometimes also dichotomized by Sapir in terms of whether the majority
or the minority of North American languages exhibit the category in
question – e.g. GENDER distinguishing masculine-feminine-neuter (minority of native languages) and gender distinguishing animate-inanimate
(widespread); NUMBER for plural distinguished from singular in noun or
even in verb vs. languages with 'no true plurals' (frequently), or with a
distributive (by reduplication) instead of a true plural (by affixation);
TENSE in languages with elaborate temporal discriminations (as four
preterits), or with 'aoristic' or indefinite tense (no discrimination between
present and past). This display of variety in CASE, GENDER, NUMBER,
and TENSE serves Sapir as a preface to show 'how a simple English sentence [*he will give it to you*] is structurally rendered into some half
dozen selected languages ... [Wishram, Takelma, Southern Paiute,
Yana, Nootka, Navajo] with attention to a few important grammatical
categories that are either not expressed at all [i.e. not formally] in languages nearer home or are expressed only fragmentarily or by implica-
tion'. Other grammatical categories, not included in the prefatory
remarks, are subsequently identified – e.g. in Nootka MODAL paradigms
and ASPECT (durative, inceptive, momentaneous, graduative (cp. Eng.
progressive), pregraduative, iterative, inceptive).

Before Bloomfield (1933), attempts were made to solve semantic
problems, but each problem was approached from the morphemic shape
of some constituent in the word – less often constituents of the sentence
(though modal particles were understood to be semantically recalcitrant).
After Bloomfield, the renaissance of semantic interest brings us back to a
reconsideration of grammars written under Boas' and Sapir's influence,

but the new approach to semantics is not now restricted to meanings marked by constituents of a word; modal particles are found to offer especially intriguing problems: in some languages, as constituents of a single-clause or multi-clause sentence; in Hopi the semantic scope of modal particles often extends to clauses adjacent to the clause in which the particle occurs. And languages that lack relative clause pronouns (e.g. English *that, which, who*) can be shown to have embedded relative clauses nevertheless.

The following sparse sample of semantic problems strives to exemplify this, and also the fresh interest in searching for underlying semantic commonalities (semantic representations?) of polysemous constituents of words or sentences (rather than to exemplify either typical semantic problems so far encountered in American Indian languages, or the extremes of their 'bewildering variety').

POLYSEMY VS. HOMOPHONY IN YAVAPAI

Kendall (1975) shows that there are underlying semantic commonalities for the /-k/ that is suffixed to nouns and the /-k/ that is suffixed to verbs, just as there are for the /-m/ that is suffixed to nouns and the /-m/ that is suffixed to verbs. The privileges of occurrence are such that in most environments where /-k/ is possible /-m/ is also; but what is crucial to the opposing claims which follow can best be stated in two steps. First, just as multiple meanings must be assigned to /-k/, so also other multiple meanings must be assigned to /-m/; second, /-k/ and /-m/ are semantically contrastive in every environment in which they can be paired.

The pre-Kendall claim was for homophony: /-k/ and /-m/ were not taken to be two paired morphemes; instead each was assumed to represent phonological convergence from different morphemes that happen to be pronounced in the same way – e.g. for Walapai it was claimed that there were five different /-k/'s, and four different /-m/'s. (The /-k/, /-m/ pairing is found in all three Pai dialects – Walapai and Havasupai as well as Yavapai – as well as in most other Yuman languages separated from the Pai dialects by language barriers.)

The earlier claim just outlined accounts for the multiple meanings of each of the paired morphemes, but without accounting for the fact that a given meaning has a parallel but different meaning for the morpheme it is paired with in the same environment. For Yavapai, as for other natural languages, it can be said that though "the number of homophonous

formatives is negligible when compared to the language's total lexicon",
the possibility of several paired homophonous formatives occurring in
several different environments seems to be distinctly unnatural. Yet this
represents the pre-Kendall claim for Pai dialects.

There is no question that multiple meanings must be assigned to each
of the two morphemes in question for Yavapai. Only some of the polysemous assignments and a small selection from the exemplifying sentences
are given in the following paragraphs.

The locative-directional marker /-k/ is glossed *toward*, in terms of a
point of reference which is THE SPEAKER. (Sentence translations are given
in full in Kendall – and her sentence numbering is preserved here –
but we do not gloss each morpheme; only one Yavapai word is cited
parenthetically and glossed – namely that of a word with one of the
paired morphemes attached.)

(1) *They came out of the house* (ʔwa·-v-k, *house-demons-from*), with
reference to the speaker who is presupposed to be outside the house
mentioned when he utters this sentence (1). However, when he says the
following sentence, the presupposition is that he is inside the house
mentioned.

(2) *They went out of my house* (ʔ-ñ-wa·-m, *my-possessive-house-from*),
with reference to the speaker, now inside rather than outside the house,
as in (1). Had the speaker said (2) while being outside the house as those
leaving the house were coming toward him, he would have said the word
for house (/ʔ-ñ-wa-/) with final /-k/ instead of final /-m/.

Other sentences exemplifying /-m/ suffixed to nouns as a case marker
designate a category called 'associational', which has an instrumental
function (e.g. *X ate corn with her hands*) or a commitative function (e.g.
X and Y ate the bread, which can also be expressed by saying that *X
ate the bread with Y*).

The question remains as to whether the 'associational' meaning of
/-m/, suffixed to nouns, is semantically related to the directional-locative
meaning of /-m/, and, if so, combinable 'into the same morpheme' or
separable as two different morphemes with the same surface shape.

The answer to the question just mentioned must await more 'critical
evidence' than is now available. This and some other alternatives for
still additional meanings of the /-k/, /-m/ pair are less relevant to the
crucial claim which is concerned with showing the meanings of /-k/
and /-m / as nominal case suffixes are semantically related to their meanings as verbal suffixes.

Their central meanings as verbal suffixes were discovered by Margaret

Langdon for one of the Yuman languages (Diegueño), and hold for the other known Yuman languages, including Yavapai. In Yavapai, some meanings of /-k/ and /-m/, as verbal suffixes, are expressed in terms of a rule called 'progressive referent switching' – i.e. for /-m/; the converse of the rule applies to /-k/.

In Yavapai, "/-k/ indicates same subject ... /-m/ different subject ... sameness or difference with regard to the next highest verb ...".

(13) *When you were sick and dreaming of bad things, I held your hands* (m-čira·v-k, *you-[be sick]*-PROX; m-tisma·č-m, *you dream*-OBV; your-hand-demons I-hold-completive).

(For Uto-Aztecan languages, we used to say – as in the *Tübatulabal Grammar* – 'non-identical actor' instead of 'progressive referent switching', but now we call the marker for progressive referent switching obviative (OBV), as in the section on Hopi, pp. 90ff. In contrast to obviative, proximate (PROX) markers indicate the sameness of subject ('identical actor') for successive clauses.)

Parallels to this kind of sentence – with PROX for same subject as subject of following clause, and OBV for not the same subject as subject of following clause – are probably not limited to languages in the Yuman and Uto-Aztecan families. But the Uto-Aztecan PROX and OBV suffixes appear in interrogative, modal, and negative sentences while they do not in Yavapai. There is a general absence of /-k/'s and /-m/'s 'when a construction is negative or interrogative' – not to mention other restrictions on /-k/ and /-m/ in other Yavapai constructions.

Some apparent exceptions 'to the reference switching operation' are restrictions which can be explained in terms of a contrast between factive verbs and non-factive verbs (i.e., verbs which do not presuppose that their complements are true). The semantic set marked by /-k/ is made up of non-factive verbs that 'are cognitive or emotional, or they are concerned with reports, questions, pleas and promises'; and besides non-factives, 'purposive and intentional constructions are also /-k/ -marked'. What these verbs have in common is that they are SPEAKER-CENTERED. Note again that the locative-directional marker /-k/ means, in effect, TOWARD THE SPEAKER.

The concluding argument in Kendall is that the contrast between factive /-m/ and non-factive /-k/ 'is related to the nominal case-marking /-m/, /-k/ contrast' by parallel shifts in the POINT OF VIEW OF THE SPEAKER: /-k/ is SPEAKER CENTERED while /-m/ is OTHER-THAN-SPEAKER CENTERED ('things at a distance, moving away from or separated conceptually from speaker'). Hence, the case-marking contrast can be related to the factive/ non-factive contrast by virtue of their reduction to two meanings for /-k/ and two meanings for /-m/, depending on whether /-k/ or /-m/ is suffixed to a verb ('indicating sameness or difference of referent from clause to clause') or suffixed to a noun ('indicating something about the speaker's perceptions, judgments or evaluations').

This argument is reasonably well supported, but that is not its main attraction, for it does not much matter whether an opposing homophony argument will eventually appeal to Yumanists more than the Kendall argument for polysemy of just two paired morphemes with many meanings (however reducible) for each. What is fascinating is the bearing of this non-homophony argument on cognitive anthropology and its relevance to linguistic theory – e.g. Postal's 'remind' (1970) as representative of generative semantics – in favor of homophony – versus Bollinger's reply in *Language* (1971) – in favor of polysemy in respect to 'remind'. Relevant to cognitive anthropology is Kendall's penultimate statement: "So long as he stays on the same subject or talks about the same subject he [the Yavapai speaker] stays in one 'conceptual location'." (Her 'conceptual location' and our 'presuppositional culture space' are not unrelated.)

(See now the New Guinea language in which one set of deictics is used when spatial reference is to the same location in which the speakers are speaking, while another set of deictics appears in sentences whose spatial reference is located in a valley or on a ridge away from the location of the speakers. This is reported in *Anthropological Linguistics* by Lawrence (AL 14. 311-16).)

VERBS WITH INCLUDED NOUNS IN ALGONQUIAN, IROQUOIS, AND UTO-AZTECAN

In his inaugural paper – not for occupying a professorial chair, but for launching a new journal (*IJAL*) – Franz Boas (1917) touched upon the possible pitfall of attributing similarities between languages to common descent when diffusion within an area might account for the similarities – whether phonetic or morphological. For the latter he says that "the incorporation of the nominal object, which in former times was considered one of the most characteristic features of American languages, is confined to certain areas, while it is foreign to others". These areas are not identified. Are they polysynthetic areas? One has the vague impression that the more polysynthetic a language is, the more frequently such noun incorporation is apt to occur. Less frequently, even in nonpolysynthetic English we find 'baby-sitter', 'man-eater' and also 'man-eating' (when the underlying verb is nominalized); even less frequently for English, the underlying verb appears as a surface verb, as in 'charcoal-broil'.

And it can furthermore be said as a matter of evidence that there are, irrespective of area, some language families in which the inclusion of nouns in verbs is possible and more or less productive for all or most languages in the family – e.g. Algonquian, Iroquoian, Uto-Aztecan – thereby raising the question of common descent instead of invoking Boas' areal linguistics. Though most languages in the first two families – Algonquian and Iroquoian – are located in the Eastern area, Uto-Aztecan languages are found scattered on a north-south axis over several different culture areas on the western side of the continent.

Michelson (1917) states that instead of 'incorporation of nominal object' occurring in Fox, an Algonquian language, he finds 'loose composition wherein the objective noun is in the midst of a verbal complex'. To avoid further controversy over the proper usage of 'noun incorporation', the present discussion is concerned with any kind of noun that is included in any kind of verb. (This permits us also to mention the parallel verb-verb compounds.)

We are now working with Jerry Boling in eliciting paired Shawnee sentences – one with the noun included in the verb beside a source sentence in which the noun is a separate word from the verb. It is as though one could say in English either *I-touched-nose-him*, as one word, or *I-touched-him on-his-nose* as two words. The semantic problem is whether there is any difference in meaning between the source sentence and the sentence or 'sentence word' with noun included in verb.

One subset of the problem, as it appears to us in Shawnee, can be formally identified. First, there are a number of verbs for which the order of constituents is (personal pronoun prefix)-(verb)-(included noun)-(inflectional suffixes); all of these verbs occur also in sentences as verbs without included nouns. Second, only certain nouns are includable.

The rest of this section gives examples which strongly suggest that we have not yet solved the semantic problem.

The subset of verbs seems to be limited to specific kinds of actions or states such as touching, bending, breaking, washing, biting, dirtying (transitive) or bent, broken, dirty (intransitive). Nouns which are includable in verbs such as those indicated are limited to body-part terms and then only (mainly?) to basic body terms (i.e. unanalyzable ones, in the sense of Berlin and Kay's *Basic Color Terms*).

An example of a verb with and without included noun follows:

(1a)   nipeʔšena hočaaši
       I touch it his nose
       I touch his nose

(1b)   nipeʔšena hočaaleki
       I touch him on his nose

(1c)   nipeʔšičaaleena
       I touch nose him (literally), but all speakers agree the meaning of
       (1c) is *I tweaked his nose.*

The source sentences (1a) and (1b), with external noun, differ mainly in
whether the locative suffix is attached to hočaale- as in (1b) but not in(1a).
In (1c), with included noun, Shawnee speakers are aware of specialization
in touching – touching in passing or by a brushing movement of hands
(i.e., by tweaking).

Otherwise there is disagreement among the several speakers we have
worked with. One speaker detected a difference between many paired
sentences – PERMANENT versus TEMPORARY condition; for example:

(2a)   nitaašiteewileče
       I have crossed (grown together) fingers

(2b)   nitaašteʔšimaaki nilečeeki
       I crossed them   my fingers
       meaning that for a moment, *I crossed my fingers.*

When another speaker was confronted with (2a) and (2b), he claimed that
he did not detect the distinction of permanent for (2a) and temporary for
(2b). Instead a quite different distinction was invoked – between being
WIDESPREAD over the body-part in question, as in (3b) and (4b), or being
LOCALIZED as in (3a) and (4a) following.

(3a)   hoθaawiθi   niškaša
       it is yellow my fingernail
       My fingernail is yellow.

(3b)   nooθaawikaše
       I have yellow fingernails.

(4a)   noomeki ninepaaka
       I am sore my elbow
       (This is ambiguous: My elbow is sore; I have a sore on my elbow.)

(4b)   noomekipaakane
       I have sore elbows or I have sores all over my elbow.

The final distinction here is that between a CHRONIC or PROLONGED condition, as in (5b) – which need not be permanent, versus TEMPORARY condition, as in (5a).

(5a) nipesiipi ninepaaka
      I am itchy my one elbow
      My elbow itches.

(5b) ninepešiipipaakane
      I have itchy elbows (as a chronic condition)

In her paper on noun incorporation in Onondaga, Hanni Woodbury (1975) gives the general rule 'that a transitive verb may incorporate its object and an intransitive verb its subject' – but for Onondaga and other northern Iroquoian languages (on the authority of Chafe) "it is in all cases the patient noun which may be incorporated".

In (1a), following, the noun is external to the verb while in (1b) the noun is included in the verb: the noun root (-yɛʔkw-) precedes the verb root (-hninu-):

(1a) waʔhahninú?   ne?   oyéʔkwa?
      tns-he/it-buy-asp   nm. prtc.   it-tobacco-n. s.
      He bought the tobacco.

(1b) waʔhayɛʔkwahní:nu?
      tns-he/it-tobacco-buy-asp
      He bought tobacco.

In the second pair of sentences, the noun again may be external to the verb (2a) or included in the verb (2b); but the verb is intransitive in both sentences.

(2a) kahihwí   ne?   ohsahéʔta?
      it-spill-cs-asp   nm.prtc.   it-bean(s)-n. s.
      The beans are spilled.

(2b) kahsaheʔtahíhwi
      it-bean(s)-spill-cs-asp
      Beans are spilled.

As a general tendency, subject to exceptions, "a noun which is incorporated makes a more general reference" – as *he bought tobacco* (1b), *beans are spilled* (2b) – than a noun which is not included in the verb – as *he bought the tobacco* (1a), *the beans are spilled* (2a). The general tendency noted is not due exclusively to the inclusion of the noun in the verb but rather 'due to the interaction of several processes' to which the bulk of Woodbury's paper is devoted.

When Wilhelm von Humboldt (1825, 1836) added an incorporating type to the early nineteenth century typology he did so to classify American Indian languages which were incorporating when "... the verb object is found in the same word as the verb-root". To von Humboldt these were languages with 'sentence words' (Greenberg, 1973:168). The usual textbook example from Uto-Aztecan is the single Nahuatl word for *I-meat-eat*.

Verbs with included nouns in Hopi also occur in sentences in which the noun is not the object of the verb; and 'sentence words' may occur without an included noun. We have worked with a number of Hopi speakers and none of them were able to specify what the semantic difference is between paired sentences – between verb with included noun and noun outside the verb – but it appears for certain culture domains that only those nouns mentioned with some frequency are includable in verbs, whether as verb object, or as bearing some other case relationship to the verb. This is especially clear in examples in which the verb object is included in verbs; hence more of such examples, following, are cited than examples of other cases determined by verbs.

E.g. verb object that is incorporated:

(1) ʔítam meló.ni-t   ʔaníwnaya
     We   melon-OBJ.   grow-CAUSE-pl.
     We raised melons.   (*melons* is external object)

(2) ʔítam melón ʔaníwnaya
     We raised melons.   (*melons* is included in verb)

(3) nɨʔ pí·ktani ʔó:vi ʔas ɨm ʔinɨŋem ʔáw qöycap-wɨ·tani
     I'm going to make piki (pi·ktani) but on account of being without
     confidence (ʔo:vi ʔas) will you add the ashes in it = will you ash-
     pour (qöycap-wɨ·tani) for me.

(4) nɨʔ qa·ʔöt hɨhmeʔ pɨt ʔaw qöycapkʷivitani
     When I shell (hɨhmeʔ, PROX in -eʔ) corn, I'll make hominy = boil
     ashes in it.

(5) tɨ·va *pinyon nut*; poŋ- *gather* pl. obj.):
     ya hákim tiva-vo·poŋ-wis-ŋʷɨ
     Who (QUESTION ones) usually go to gather pinyon nuts?

(6) (kitɨk-ta *he roasts it*):
     ʔitam tiva-ktɨk-tota-t pɨʔ mirɨknayat pɨʔ ason wɨ:wihi-yani
     We roast pinyons (PROX in -t, pl. subj., pf.), then we grind (them)
     lightly, then later we'll do the winnowing.

(7)   (qané·lo *sheep* mí:na *he kills it*):
ʔítam qanélminayani ʔitam pit ʔiŋwayat monsiltotani
We will kill a sheep and we will make its blood sausage.

(8)   niváyoyoki it's snowing (snow-raining)

(9)   lemówyoyoki it's hailing (hail-raining)

E.g. cases other than verb object, as incorporated instrumental or locative, etc.; or, most rarely, compounds including two verbs, of which one is incorporated:

(10)   (tö·vi *charcoal*, ti:pe *broil*):
ya hak hi·ta tövi-tpe-ʔŋʷi
What (OBJ) does one charcoal-broil?

(11)   (kʷá:hi *eagle*, yáqa *nose*, móki *die*):
kʷa:yaqmoki-wta *he's got a runny nose*

(12)   (naka *hot sand*, ʔá:ma *he buries it*):
piʔ hak pit nak-ʔam-ŋʷi
Then one cooks it by burying it in hot sand = one hot sand-buries it.

(13)   tamá:tiy-va he's starting to have a toothache

(14)   ponó-titiya he's got a stomachache

(15)   (timálaʔat *his work*, ti:va *he drops, throws sg. obj.*):
timál-tiva he fired him

(16)   (hópi *Hopi (person)*, yiʔáʔatá *he talks, makes speech,* ti:qayi *he learns, listens*):
hopí-yiʔáʔata he's talking Hopi

(17)   hopí:-titiqayi he's learning Hopi

(18)   honán-wiŋʷa he belongs to Badger clan

(19)   ʔís-wiŋʷa he's Coyote clan

(20)   (pölaviki *bread*, tiwiʔyta *he knows (has knowledge of) it*):
ya ʔim pölaviktiwiʔyta Do you know how to make bread?

(21)   (mákma *go hunt*, píti *he arrives*, with suppletive plural ʔöki *they arrive*):
pám mák-viti *he arrives from hunting (hunt-arrive)*;
píma mák-ʔökiyaqáʔe ʔovi *because they arrive from hunting* ...

EMBEDDED SENTENCES IN HOPI

All sentences in Hopi contain at least one independent mode clause.
Sentences may also include non-independent mode clauses. These non-
independent mode clauses are formed in two ways: by a nominalizing
suffix /-qa/ or by a conjunct mode suffix (from a set of six such suffixes).
The central point of this discussion of Hopi will be to explore such semantic commonalities as may exist between nominalized constructions in
/-qa/ and conjunct mode constructions.

As is well known, Hopi (like other Uto-Aztecan languages) conjoins
clauses by the use of a suffix which distinguishes whether the subject of the
conjunct mode clause is the same or different than the subject of the
following clause. The conjunct mode suffix which marks obviative
(OBV), /-q/, indicates that the following clause has a different subject;
on the other hand, a proximate (PROX) mode conjunct suffix – /-qaʔe/
is the one treated in this paper – indicates that the following clause has
the same subject as that of the proximate mode clause.

Though it is true that the distinction between obviative and proximate
is shared by the conjunct mode suffixes, as mentioned, and clauses formed
by the nominalizing suffix /-qa/ treated below, the latter do not have a
conjoining function. Conjunct mode clauses are unique in combining the
obviative-proximate distinction with the conjoining function.

Sentences which are nominalized by final /-qa/ may serve the usual
functions of nouns. Thus, /moːtitaqa/ *the winner* is a nominalization of
/moːtita/ *he is first* (as in a foot race) and appears as subject in the
sentence

yaw moːtitaqa yatkinat maqiwni
The winner will be given a saddle.

In addition to appearing in sentences as single word noun phrases as *the
winner* in the sentence preceding, nominalizations in /-qa/ (plus or minus
case and number suffixes) may have as their scope a sentence of several
words. Thus, the sentence *Those boys will receive the paper* is nominalized
and serves as possessor of what is inflected as *their names* (tiŋʷiniʔam)
in the following sentence.

ʔima toːtim titivenit kʷisiyaniqamiy tiŋʷiniʔam pay pa·s peʔyiŋʷa
*The names of those boys who will receive the paper are carefully written
down.*

This nominalization function of /-qa/ is not shared by conjunct mode
constructions, which serve no nominalization function whatever.

When a nominalization in /-qa/ is in apposition to a head noun, it serves as a relative clause, which incidentally shows concordance of case and number between the head noun and the relative clause nominalized in /-qa/.

Relative clauses on singular nouns in object case distinguish OBV vs. PROX by the selection of one of two different object suffixes: /-t/ in relative clauses in /-qat/ indicates an OBV relativization – i.e. the subject of the sentence relativized; (the lower sentence) is different than the subject of the matrix or higher sentence /-y/ in relative clauses in /-qay/ indicates a PROX relativization – i.e. the subject of the sentence relativized (the lower sentence) is the same as the subject of the matrix or higher sentence.

The following shows an OBV relative clause, the subject of which (*the old woman*) is different than the subject of the matrix sentence (*I*, in in *I asked the old woman*).

kɨr nɨʔ soʔwɨ·tit sipalat moyoyotaqat tɨ·viŋta
I asked the old woman who is gumming peaches.

Such relative clauses may also be postposed to the matrix sentence (instead of occurring immediately after the head noun as above). The next example shows such postposing: the matrix sentence (*I threw out the beans*) precedes the OBV relative clause (*it* [object noun of matrix pronominalized] *you burned yesterday*):

nɨʔ ʔöŋavat maspa pɨt ʔɨm ta·vok taqcokqat
I threw out the beans which you burned yesterday.

The following sentence is a contrastive parallel to the preceding sentence, namely a PROX relative clause, marked as PROX by the object suffix /-y/ (rather than /-t/) after the nominalizing suffix /-qa/. The matrix sentence (*I threw out my beans*) precedes the PROX relative clause (*it* [pronominalized object of the matrix] *burned yesterday*).

nɨʔ ʔiʔöŋavay maspa pɨt ta·vok taqcokqay
I threw out my beans which I burned yesterday.

Here the subject of the PROX relative clause is not repeated; it is implicitly marked by the PROX /-y/ to be the same as the subject of the matrix sentence.

It has been claimed that relative clauses are derived from conjoined sentences; relevant to this claim is the fact that some conjunct mode clauses in Hopi serve as relative clauses. All conjunct mode clauses make the distinction between OBV and PROX whether they function as conjoining clauses or as relative clauses.

The following shows an OBV relative clause in conjunct mode (marked by /-q/) to show that the subject of the relative clause *(beans)* is different than the subject of the matrix sentence *(people* in *people just do not have beans)*.

hakim ʔöŋavat hinʔir ci·votniq pay qa pityaŋʷi.
People just do not have beans which are very hot.

This may be contrasted with PROX in the following sentence in which the conjunct mode suffix /-qaʔe/ marks the fact that the subject of the relative clause *(I* in *which I tore)* is the same as the subject of the matrix sentence *(I* in *I sewed back up my shirt)*.

niʔ ʔinapnay ʔahoy ʔaw ti·ʔiha niʔ pit ci·kaqaʔe
I sewed back up my shirt which I tore.

Here the subject – /niʔ/ for *I* – is repeated in the relative clause; such repetition is optional.

A relatively small set of Hopi verbs such as the verbs for *say, tell, ask as a question, ask as a favor, instruct, remember* and *remind, believe, know, want, see,* and *hear*, appear with sentence complements. At least two kinds of sentential complement construction are found in Hopi: one kind is formed with nominalizations in /-qa/; the other kind is formed with conjunct mode suffixes. In both kinds of complements the distinction between OBV and PROX is morphologically indicated.

The same case suffixes which show the OBV-PROX contast on relative clauses in /-qa/ are used for the OBV-PROX distinction of complements in /-qa/. Hopi always commits itself for complements in /-qa/ in respect to being PROX or OBV because such complements are only singular; they are never marked with noun plural suffixes as relative clauses may be.

The illustrative pair of sentences following show the same matrix sentence *(you should tell him)*. To this matrix complements are preposed.

The complement for the first sentence (*"you made it"* – a direct quotation) is OBV because the *you* of the matrix refers to the person addressed, while the *you* of the complement refers to another person – a third person that the addressee is instructed to tell. This first sentence could be paraphrased in Hopi to read *you should tell him that he made it*.

ʔim pit yikiqat ʔim ʔaw paŋqawni
You should tell him "You made it" [i.e. *he made it*]

The complement for the second sentence (*you made it* – but not a direct quotation) is PROX because the subject of the matrix sentence *(you)* and the subject of the complement *(you)* are coreferential.

ʔɨm pɨt yɨkɨqay ʔɨm ʔaw paŋqawɨ
You should tell him you made it.

Conjunct mode suffixes which make the OBV-PROX contrast both in conjoining and in relative clauses are in addition used in sentential complements, where they again make the OBV-PROX contrast.

   The illustrative pair of sentences below share a single matrix sentence
(I don't remember). To this an OBV complement and a PROX complement,
respectively, are postposed. The subject of the OBV complement is explicitly given in Hopi – /ʔɨm/ for *you* – because it refers to a different person
than the subject person of the matrix sentence – *I*. Though not explicitly
repeated in Hopi, the subject of the PROX complement *(I)* is taken to be
the same as the subject of matrix sentence *(I)*, as indicated by the PROX
suffix – /-qaʔe/.

nɨʔ qa ʔiʔiniʔyta haqam ʔɨm pɨt tavɨq
I don't remember where you put it.

nɨʔ qa ʔiʔiniʔyta haqam pɨt tavɨqaʔe
I don't remember where I put it.

Another use of conjunct mode clauses is as adverbial clauses – time
adverbials and some modal adverbials. A curious feature of these
conjunct mode adverbial clauses is the fact their subjects, when specified,
are always in object case. The time adverbials in the following pair of
sentences distinguish between OBV and PROX respectively.

   In the first sentence, exemplifying an OBV time adverbial, the object of
the matrix sentence *(did he pay you)* is not a pivot which also serves as the
subject *(you)* of the time adverbial *(when you chanted)* because the
verb for *pay* in Hopi calls for an indirect object – /ɨ·mi/ for *to you*.
Here, in the surface sentence, the time adverbial clause is embedded
between the Hopi words for *did he* and *pay to you*.

ya pam ʔɨŋ caʔcaʔlawq ʔɨmi sisvi
Did he pay you when you chanted?

In the next sentence, the subject of the time adverbial clause *(I* in *when
I was five years old)* appears in the inflectional form for object case in
Hopi (niy); the literal reading is *When me was five years old ...* . On the
other hand, the subject of the matrix sentence *(I* in *I broke my arm)*
appears in the usual inflectional form for subject case in Hopi (nɨʔ).

niy civot ya·saŋʷiniʔytaqaʔe nɨʔ ʔimay qöhikna
When I was five years old I broke my arm.

The subject referent of PROX lower sentences is indicated (by a PROX suffix) to be the same person referent as the subject of the matrix sentence, though it is possible to repeat the subject of the matrix sentence in the PROX lower sentence. When the subject is not repeated in the PROX lower sentence, the sentential result may be curiously ambiguous. Consider now the following sentence which, in structure, is triply ambiguous.

ʔöŋava hinir kʷalalaʔykɨqaʔe ʔaŋq wehebeʔykɨ
beans hard boiling-PROX from it spilled over

The literal word by word glosses of this sentence can be interpreted to reflect three structural readings –either a conjoined sentence without causality *(The beans had been boiling hard and boiled over)*; or a conjoined sentence in which the PROX clause *(Because the beans had been boiling hard)* bears a causal relationship to the following independent mode clause *(they boiled over)*. Or else the PROX clause may be interpreted as a relative clause, the head noun of which is *beans* (subject of the matrix sentence; in this interpretation, the relative clause *(which had been boiling hard)* is embedded in the matrix sentence *(beans boiled over)*.

This makes two structural ambiguities: PROX clause as conjoined with independent clause, and PROX clause as a relative clause that is embedded in the independent matrix sentence. The third structural ambiguity results when the PROX clause is interpreted to be a time adverbial clause *(when they had been boiling hard)* that is embedded in the matrix sentence *(beans boiled over)*.

In sum, though the sentence in question is structurally ambiguous, the semantic interpretations derived from the multiple structures overlap. Such sentences, as the above, lend support to the claims for a semantic connection between relative clauses and conjoined clauses.

A salient language-linked or language-particular semantic commonality among the types of sentence construction cited above is the paired opposition that exists between obviative or switch-reference and proximate or same-reference.

Though these contrasts of the Uto-Aztecan type are known for other American Indian language families, they are in general associated with conjoined sentences only rather than, as in Hopi, also with relative clauses and sentential complements.

Some constraints on the occurrence of some relativizations can be explained in terms of the occasional failure of the OBV-PROX distinction. There is a constraint on relative clauses formed with /-qa/ in subject case – namely on relative clauses of which the head noun is subject of the higher sentence; such relative clauses can only be PROX. Subjects in Hopi are marked by the absence of object or locational case suffixes. The distinction between OBV and PROX in noun morphology is made possible by the object case suffixes; hence when the object case suffixes are lacking, as they are in the subject case, the relative clause cannot be marked for the OBV-PROX distinction. Lacking a formal way of marking this distinction, Hopi restricts the occurrence of relative clauses on the subject head noun to PROX. In other words, the coreferential noun phrase of the lower relativized sentence – a NP which is deleted under identity with the subject NP (the head noun) of the higher sentence – must be in subject case.

Furthermore, the marking of the distinction between OBV and PROX for /-qa/ relative clauses in object case (as illustrated above) is possible only for singular relative clauses in apposition with singular head nouns. It is impossible to show this distinction on object plural relative clauses which are marked only by /-qamiy/ rather than by a pair of suffixes to maintain the distinction which is maintained on object singular relative clauses marked /-qat/ for OBV, /-qay/ for PROX, i.e. object plural relative clauses do not distinguish OBV from PROX.

Various facets of Hopi syntax conspire to make perfectly clear the identification of the subject of a complex sentence. Thus, on the one hand, embedded sentences which can come between the subject of a higher sentence and its verb – as time adverbials and some complements – have their subjects marked for object case; on the other hand, embedded sentences which have subject nouns in subject case are preposed or postposed to the higher sentence, so that no subject noun phrase intervenes between a subject and its verb. When this cannot be avoided – as when doubly embedded sentences intervene – or whenever several words intervene between the sentence-initial subject and the sentence-final verb, as in sentences like

pam ta·qa ʔitamɨmi paŋqawqa yaw ʔitam wɨ·haq si·vat ʔöma:taniqat pam hin ʔɨr ʔacata
The man who told us we'd gets lots of money was lying,

The subject of the higher sentence may be repeated in pronominalized form before its verb; a more literal translation of this Hopi sentence would be

The man who told us we'd get lots of money he was lying.

the persistent OBV-PROX contrast in the Hopi expression of conjoined sentences with conjunct mode clauses, and in relative clauses and complements – whether derived by nominalization in /-qa/ or by conjunct mode marking – can accordingly be said to be at the center of the conspiracy to clarify the semantic-syntactic identification of subjects in complex Hopi sentences.

Indiana University

REFERENCES

Bloomfield, L. 1933. Language. New York: Holt, Rinehart and Winston.
Boas, F. 1911. Introduction to the Handbook of American Indian languages, ed. by F. Boas, 1-83. Bureau of American Ethnology Bulletin 40 Part. Washington D.C.: Smithsonian Institution 1917.
—. 1917. Introductory. International Journal of American Linguistics 1.1-8.
Bolinger, D. 1971. Semantic overloading: A restudy of the verb 'remind'. Language 47.522-47.
Davis, P. W. 1973. Modern theories of language. Englewood Cliffs, New Jersey: Prentice Hall.
Greenberg, J. 1973. Typological classification. Current Trends in Linguistics 11.168.
Hale, K. 1973. The role of American Indian linguistics in bilingual education. Bilingualism in the Southwest, ed. by P. R. Turner. Tucson: University of Arizona Press.
—. 1975. Theoretical linguistics in relation to American Indian communities. American Indian Languages and American Linguistics, ed. by W. L. Chafe, 35-50. Lisse: The Peter de Ridder Press.
Kendall, M. B. 1975. The /-k/, /-m/ problem in Yavapai syntax. International Journal of American Linguistics.
Labov, W. 1972. Sociolinguistic patterns. Philadelphia: University of Pennsylvania Press.
Lawrence, H. 1972. Viewpoint and location in Oksapmin. Anthropological Linguistics 14.311-16.
Michelson, T. 1917. Notes on Algonkian languages. International Journal of American Linguistics 1.50-57.
Postal, P. 1970. On the surface verb remind. Linguistic Inquiry 1.37-120. Reprinted in Studies in Linguistic Semantics, ed. by C. J. Fillmore and D. T. Langendoen, 1971. New York: Holt, Rinehart and Winston.
Rappaport, R. A. 1967. Pigs for the ancestors: A ritual in the ecology of the New Guinea people. New Haven: Yale University Press.
Robins, R. H. 1974. Language. Encyclopaedia Britannica, 15th edition, 10,642-62.
Sapir, E. 1917. Review of Het identificeerend karakter der possesieve flexie in talen van Noord-Amerika by C. C. Uhlenbeck. International Journal of American Linguistics 1.86-90.
—. 1929. American Indian grammatical categories, ed. by M. Swadesh. Word 2.103-12. Reprinted in Language in Culture and Society, ed. by D. Hymes, 101-11. New York: Harper and Row.
Voegelin, C. F. 1935. Tübatulabal grammar. University of California Publications in American Anthropology and Ethnology 34.55-190.
—., F. M. Voegelin, and LaVerne Masayesva Jeanne. Forthcoming. Hopi semantics. Handbook of American Indian languages. Washington D.C.: Smithsonian Institution.

Whorf, B. L. 1946. The Hopi language, Toreva dialect. Linguistic Structures of Native America, ed. by H. Hoijer. Viking Fund Publications in Anthropology 6.
Woodbury, H. 1975. Onodaga noun incorporation: Some notes on the interdependence of syntax and semantics. International Journal of American Linguistics 41.10-20.

NOTES

[1] This paper was read and discussed at the Ethnolinguistic Seminar in Bloomington as well as at the Second LSA Golden Anniversary Symposium in Berkeley. We hereby acknowledge with thanks the benefit we received from all those who entered into the discussion at the Seminar and at the Symposium; for fresh insights we were especially stimulated by Charles Bird, Fred Householder, Kenneth Hale, Wallace Chafe, Einar Haugen, and the official LSA discussant, Ronald Langacker.

[2] We have often commented on the spotty nature of awareness in the unawareness landscape of untrained native speakers. All Hopi speakers we have worked with think we will not realize, as they realize, how plural agent of verbs is distinguished from dual agent; yet the same speakers seem often unaware of the way plural nouns are distinguished from dual and paucal nouns. But awareness may not be deeply buried, as Hale argues. Whatever the depth of unawareness, and however spotty the untrained speaker's knowledge of his native language may be, it is, as we interpret the literature, taken for granted that the trained speaker – i.e. the linguist – is aware of the grammar of his native language; but how about the anthropological linguist who also claims awareness of the language he analyzes – the non-native language of which he is capable of little speaking-ability and less understanding-ability (or the other way around)? Both can be said to be aware of the phonology and the constituents of the syntax in greater detail than the non-linguist native speaker. If both are genuinely aware of the language-linked semantics of the languages they study, why is it that linguists working on the same native language differ among each other about semantic representations or the interpretations of them? And why did anthropological linguists defer comprehensive consideration of semantics in the middle third of this century? Not to leave these questions dangling rhetorically, let us agree that both the non-linguist's and the linguist's awareness of semantics is spotty, but that the illuminated spots occur in different places.

(Boas stressed the partial non-awareness by non-linguists of language-linked semantics in the languages they speak; now Lévi-Strauss claims even more non-awareness of culture-linked semantics of *persons-in-the-culture*, and he claims that the central task of the anthropologist is to detect the unconscious meanings in the culture he is investigating.)

[3] This opens up new vistas for investigation – for one example, are different types of grammar recoverable at different depths of awareness? For another example, does the near-surface awareness, which is found among Navajo children, atrophy beyond the end of childhood?

[4] Leonard Bloomfield once fantasied what an ideal grammar would be like; it would be one which eschewed the usual generalizations of traditional grammars (now called 'rules') and in their place cited only the examples which support the rules. In effect, each 'game' that the Navajo child masters is an aspect of such an 'ideal' grammar of Navajo.

[5] This advice was repeated over and over again in Bloomfield's plenary lectures which were attended by everyone who was a student or teacher in the several Linguistic Institutes at Ann Arbor and Chapel Hill at which Bloomfield worked with imported Ojibwa informants; it was found that very explicit formal structure could be obtained

with minimum attention to semantics – or, as Davis (1973) interprets the inductive or testable work of Bloomfield, 'idea' and 'concept' and introspection in general 'are judged as an unsuitable basis for theory' (89). Bloomfield's least successful contribution to theory was his introduction of the 'sememe' and the 'tagmeme', which were generally understood at the time (after 1933) to be redundant with formal structure and hence dispensible – or, as Davis puts it, "... because such a meaning hierarchy would be isomorphic with that of grammar and the sememes isomorphic with the entries in the lexicon, the two must be made into a single one" (121).

As is well known, Bloomfield's 'tagmeme' is the forerunner of Pike's 'Tagmemic Theory' (173-216); and Bloomfield's 'sememe' is incorporated in Lamb's 'Stratificational Grammar' (301-36) – rather torturously, as Davis explains (313).

6 This expectation is naturally not mentioned by Davis (1973) since he does not include in his theories of language those of 'Boas, Sapir, nor any of those theories proposed by Russian linguists' (xi). Davis summarizes four theories associated with European linguists, and four or five American theories; that of (1) Leonard Bloomfield is made coordinate with (2) Post-Bloomfieldian Theory, (3) Tagmemic Theory, (4) Stratificational Grammar, and (5) Transformational Generative Grammar. This makes structural linguistics compartmentalized in an unjustified way. Compartmentalization may facilitate easy communication; but here it misses the generalization that the compartmentalized approaches listed, (1)-(4), all lie within a single frame of reference (structural or descriptive linguistics), while (5) occupies a really different frame of reference.

Also it does not account for the confidence felt in respect to solving semantic problems in the early pre-Bloomfieldian work with American Indian languages and the resurrection of this confidence about a decade ago when it first began to appear that the increasing diversifications within the framework of transformational grammar are not replacing structural linguistics but are, instead, absorbing it and extending it in exciting ways.

SEMANTICS OF NATIVE LANGUAGES
IN NORTH AMERICA

DISCUSSION BY RONALD W. LANGACKER

The Voegelins have presented an interesting paper that touches on many
aspects of the relation between semantic studies and the investigation of
Native American languages. This is a vast topic of central importance
for the linguistics of today and the linguistics of tomorrow. Meaning,
after all, is what language is all about, and American Indian languages
provide an ideal laboratory for the study of semantic questions and linguistic questions in general. Because of the vastness of the topic, I have
decided not to go over the Voegelins' ideas step by step – I believe their
paper speaks for itself – but rather to use them as a point of departure
for a few brief remarks on matters complementary to those they have
explicitly considered. Perhaps I should say instead that I will use them as
a point of arrival; my initial comments will be somewhat removed from
the substance of the Voegelins' paper, while my later comments will
relate more directly to matters they have discussed.

Native American languages can provide crucial insights bearing on
current meaning-related theoretical issues. They can do so both because
of their diversity and because more of their semantic structure is often
realized overtly than is sometimes the case in English and other Standard
Average European languages. Leaving aside phonology, most current
theoretical disputes are clearly meaning-related; this is especially so in
the case of the battle over generative versus interpretive semantics, as
suggested by the very names of these schools.

The debate between generative and interpretive semanticists has been
of singular sterility, largely because none of the participants seem to
realize what they are really fighting about. For example, the issue of
excessive generative power is a whale-sized red herring ('Your Turing
machine can beat up my Turing machine'), since in the absence of a
meaningful account of substantive language universals neither theory is
significantly and non-arbitrarily constrained. Moreover, however different the theories may look, in most respects they are essentially equivalent;

in particular it makes no difference whether you call your global rule a derivational constraint or a surface structure semantic interpretation rule. About the only place the two theories do differ is in their treatment of semantic structure, and in their view of the relation between semantics, syntax, and lexicon.

The notion of 'scope' is a unifying concept in the generative semantic approach to meaning. Scope, essentially, is the relation between a main clause predicate and the subordinate clause it commands; for example, in the sentence *It is possible we will lose*, the subordinate clause *we will lose* is said to be in the semantic scope of the predicate *possible*. The basic generative semantic hypothesis is that scope relations should be handled as underlying main clause-subordinate clause relations even in those instances where the elements involved are in the same surface clause. In the sentence *We may lose*, for instance, *may* is said to bear the same scope relation to *we lose* that *possible* did in the previous example. To treat scope in a uniform manner, generative semanticists posit underlying representations in which modals like *may* function as higher predicates taking a subordinate clause subject, just as *possible* does. This hypothesis leads inevitably, then, to highly abstract underlying representations in which the syntactic concept of subordination is used to explicate the semantic notion of scope. Interpretive semantics, by contrast, grudgingly recognizes scope but chooses not to integrate this notion with the syntactic notion of subordination.

American Indian languages often provide evidence that bears in one way or another on the validity of the unifying hypothesis of generative semantics. Various languages, for instance, attest to the verbal or predicate status of scope-bearing elements whose status as predicates is much less apparent and much more controversial in English and other European languages. This is the case with the marker of negation in certain Yuman languages, as argued by Carol Baker and other students of Margaret Langdon. Quantifiers, in addition to their attributive use, function overtly as predicates in a number of Uto-Aztecan languages, casting doubt on the insinuation by opponents of abstract analyses that the comparable English sentences (e.g. *His problems are many*) are marginal, archaic, stilted, or otherwise sufficiently aberrant from healthy language usage as to be unworthy and unneedful of explanation. I do not claim that such facts translate directly into conclusive evidence about the structure of English, nor do I claim that they establish generative semantics as the proper theory – no viable theory of language presently exists; I only suggest that they add considerable plausibility to the kinds of abstract semantic representations being considered and to the unifying hypothesis equating scope with subordination.

Native American languages can corroborate and even inspire other kinds of proposals regarding semantic representations. Pamela Munro, for example, has found clear and seemingly conclusive evidence – including their overt occurrence in surface structure – for positing the higher verbs *be* and *do* above stative and active sentences respectively in Mojave. This of course corroborates Ross's hypothesized *do* above active sentences in English, posited on the basis of less direct evidence, since this *do* surfaces in English only in special constructions. Also, Munro and I have independently reached the same conclusion regarding the underlying representation of passive sentences, she for Mojave and myself for Uto-Aztecan. While its applicability to English and other languages needs further investigation, we offer it for serious consideration as a universal characterization of the semantic structure of passive sentences. In our proposed underlying structure for passives, a clause with unspecified subject is embedded to the higher predicate *be*. In Mojave and a number of Uto-Aztecan languages, the underlying subject must be unspecified, since it cannot surface, even as a postpositional object; also, the construction is possible with intransitive verbs in Uto-Aztecan, yielding an impersonal construction in which no overt subject or object is possible. In Mojave, positing a higher verb *be* accounts automatically for the apparent passive marker -*č*, whose real function is seen to be that of marking the lower clause as a subject, the subject of *be*. This underlying structure, we feel, helps to explicate the meaning of passive sentences, a meaning we must properly characterize if we hope to come to grips with such phenomena as the noun-ranking that governs Navajo passives, which the Voegelins noted.

Another facet of the unifying hypothesis of generative semantics pertains to the internal structure of lexical items. The claim is made that complex lexical items, and even single morphemes, may lexicalize a complex semantic structure; in the case of verbs, this semantic structure may contain more than one predicate, with the predicates bearing scope relations to one another. In a previously published paper, I argued that the rule of predicate raising needed to make this analysis work is directly and strongly motivated for Uto-Aztecan and other exotic languages, though the motivation for English is only indirect. This is because the semantic predicates clumped together by predicate raising are often lexicalized separately in Uto-Aztecan as nested verb suffixes, with clearly defined meanings, while in English they tend, when clumped together, to all be lexicalized in a single morpheme. Uto-Aztecan provides another kind of evidence that at least some complex lexical items must be transformationally derived, a claim considered by some to be dubious. I am thinking here of numerous instances in which a derivational suffix can only reasonably be construed as applying both to the word on which it surfaces and a preceding word or phrase. For instance, a derivational suffix meaning 'have' might be found in a sentence that translates literally as *It long tail-have*, for 'It has a long tail'. *Tail-have* and the like must be transformationally derived rather than listed in the lexicon, both because the construction is fully productive and because a purely lexical approach would fail completely to account for the occurrence of modifiers such as *long* in the example cited.

Now I want to turn to another important aspect of meaning in language, one about which neither generative nor interpretive semantics has as yet had anything very cogent to say. I have in mind the related phenomena of metaphor, semantic extension, and idiomaticization. Even if one accepts the unifying hypothesis of generative semantics, a reasonable account of these phenomena remains to be achieved and remains necessary for anything approaching a full acount of meaning, not to mention syntax. For example, consider the semantic subtleties of Papago *čim*, described by Kenneth Hale, and Hopi *ʔas*, described by the Voegelins. Here the concepts of generative semantics will at best tell only part of the story. To understand the role and evolution of these and many other particles, so crucial in American Indian linguistics, we must trace the subtle semantic shifts and extensions that give rise to their varied meanings and uses. This will require us not only to elucidate semantic relationships not reducible to alternate scope relationships, such as the use of Papago *čim* for both 'try' and past tense, but also to revise our conception of grammar in some way that recognizes the naturalness and prevalence of metaphor and enables us to account nonarbitrarily for the lingering relationship between related senses and uses of a lexical item.

Metaphor, semantic extension, and idiomaticization are of course not limited to particles; they can occur with lexical units of any size, even with grammatical constructions and sentence types. Consider, for example, noun incorporation in Shawnee. The Voegelins indicated that verbs with incorporated nouns tend to indicate a chronic, prolonged, or permanent condition, in contrast to the more temporary condition designated by the periphrastic locution with a non-incorporated noun. Evidently this is not a property associated with specific verb-noun pairs –

or at least not solely with specific verb-noun pairs – but one associated with the construction per se. Or consider a reversed polarity tag question construction in Papago, used with the sense of 'because'; for instance, a sentence with the literal meaning 'He left, wasn't he tired?' is understood to mean 'He left because he was tired'. Or more generally, consider any derived lexical item whose sense is not precisely what one would predict from its component parts and manner of construction, whether due to semantic specialization, metaphorical extension, or whatever.

What should a grammar say in cases like these? I believe we must reject the simple-minded argument – which we might partially identify with strict lexicalism – that an abstract source must be rejected for a construction or lexical item if there is any appreciable semantic or syntactic difference at all between that element and its putative source. Thus, I would not necessarily reject the derivation of *kill* in English from *cause to die* solely on the basis of the differences between them that various linguists have pointed out, and I would not necessarily reject an interrogative source for Papago 'because' clauses should it be shown that they differ in certain properties from other questions. The specialized or idiomatic use of constructions or lexical items may eventually lead to reanalysis of their underlying representations so as to sever their connection, often metaphorical, with their origin and render them non-idiomatic, but precisely when that reanalysis takes place is an open question, and it is certainly simplistic to insist that it takes place at the first hint of different behavior between source and output. Such a view would in fact deny the possibility of synchronic metaphor in grammar, since metaphorical extensions necessarily imply a difference between source and output, and would fail to do justice to the intuitively obvious fact that the loss of the sense of metaphor in idiomaticization is a gradual rather than an instantaneous process. It is also difficult to see how a strict lexicalist hypothesis would handle cases, like the Shawnee and Papago examples, where a construction rather than a lexical item has taken on non-literal sense.

I might mention in passing that the syntactic form of an expression is one source of metaphor and semantic shifts. For example, the principal semantic difference between *kill* and *cause to die* – namely that *kill* tends to imply a direct and immediate relation between causation and death, a single unified process, while *cause to die* tends to imply two separate though causally related events – correlates precisely with the difference in surface form between the monomorphemic *kill* and the periphrastic *cause to die* with two overt predicates. This I believe to be no accident. Similarly, it is probably no accident that incorporated verb-noun constructions in Shawnee designate chronic or permanent conditions, while a sense of contingency is associated with the periphrastic variant in which the noun and verb are separate words, related only through the more contingent, totally nonlexical process of sentence construction.

Time prevents me from discussing these notions more fully, or from exploring the many other semantic questions raised by the Voegelins' paper. For example, any discussion of Hopi in the present context raises the issue (or specter) of the Sapir-Whorf hypothesis, to which I personally cannot subscribe, at least in any strong – and hence interesting – form.

Be that as it may, Whorf has demonstrated, and American Indian languages readily show, that different languages may encode comparable situations in radically different ways, casting serious doubt on the facile claim that semantic representations are identical for all languages and raising the almost wholly neglected issue of systematic metaphor in language, systematically different ways of encoding conceived situations in linguistic form. There is little doubt languages do differ in this way; for example, my possession of a basket would be expressed in some languages as 'I have a basket', in others as 'I have my basket', and in others as 'My basket is', and it strikes me as wrong-headed to try to reduce all of these to a single semantic representation. If time permitted, I would like to suggest that the 'associational' meaning of the Yavapai suffix -m discussed by the Voegelins is pertinent to all of these possessive locutions, being in effect their common denominator, and I would like to relate this to the core meaning of the Russian genitive case as explicated by Jakobson in a famous article. But time does not permit, so I will not.

University of California, San Diego

AMERICAN INDIAN LINGUISTICS
IN NEW SPAIN

NORMAN A. MCQUOWN

When Columbus landed on Watling's Island on October 12, 1492, and made first contact with the inhabitants of the New World, he unwittingly inaugurated a new phase in linguistic (and in cultural and in societal) studies – a phase which much later came to be labeled 'the Americanist contribution' to general linguistics (and to general anthropology). I have chosen my title with the intention of illustrating from the details of a case with which I have some personal acquaintance the appropriateness of that characterization of studies of American Indian languages (and cultures and societies).

'La Nueva España', as those who followed after Columbus came to call what we now label Mexico and Guatemala, is an area wherein such linguistic studies as were carried on may be considered as typical of similar studies carried on elsewhere: in the rest of Central America and in the Caribbean, in South America, and 'north of the border', in the rest of North America. Professional linguistic studies did not begin in New Spain until – after the conquest of Mexico by Cortés – the first Catholic missionaries began to arrive: Fray Pedro de Gante [1553] in 1523, and twelve other Franciscan friars in 1524. Early aided by Alonso de Molina [1555], a child of a Spanish widow, who learned his Nahuatl from his Indian playmates and who subsequently became a priest, the Franciscans produced, between 1524 and 1572, more than eighty grammars, dictionaries, catechisms, breviaries, and scriptural translations into the language of the Aztecs of Central Mexico, into what later came to be called CLASSICAL NAHUATL, a language which served for more than two centuries as the *lingua franca* of Spanish ministry and administration. The Dominicans, arriving in 1526, and the Augustinians in 1533, together with the Franciscans already on the scene, studied and preached, not only in NAHUATL, but also in one or more of the more than a hundred other languages spoken by other indigenous occupants of New Spain, both tributary and non-tributary to the centrally dominant Aztecs.

Between 1524 and 1572, a total of 109 known works, in (and on) HUASTEC (Cruz 1571), MATLALTZINCA (Castro 1542), MIXTEC (Fernández 1567), NAHUATL (Molina 1555), OTOMI (Vargas 1576), TARASCAN (Gilberti 1558), TOTONAC (Olmos [?]), ZAPOTEC (Feria 1567), and ZOQUE (Cepeda [?]) were produced by Franciscans, Dominicans, and Augustinians. Some of the friars were in command of (and produced works on) more than one of the indigenous languages: Fray Andrés de Olmos produced an *Arte para aprender la lengua mexicana* in 1547 (a copy of which survives in the National Library in Madrid), and is alleged to have produced similar 'Artes' on Huastec and on Totonac. Others produced multiple works on (or in) some one of the indigenous languages: Fray Maturino Gilberti produced his *Arte de la lengua de Michoacán* in 1558, his *Vocabulario* ..., his *Diálogo de doctrina christiana* ..., and his *Cartilla para los niños en lengua tarasca* in 1559, and his *Evangelios* ... in 1560. From this period, surviving *grammars* are those of Olmos (NAHUATL, 1547), Gilberti (TARASCAN, 1558), Molina (NAHUATL, 1571), Córdoba (ZAPOTEC, 1578), Reyes (MIXTEC, 1593), and Rincón (NA- HUATL, 1595), and surviving *dictionaries* are those of Molina (NAHUATL, 1555-71), Gilberti (TARASCAN, 1559), Córdoba (ZAPOTEC, 1578), and Alvarado (MIXTEC, 1593); the Córdoba, Reyes, Rincón, and Alvarado, post-dating the 1524-72 period, constitute, at the end of the sixteenth century, a new impetus to the course of the evangelization.

This new impetus lasted through the early part of the seventeenth century and produced further *grammars* [of MATLALTZINCA (Guevara 1638, Basalenque 1640), NÁHUATL (Carochi 1645), and Yucatec MAYA (Coronel 1620)] and *dictionaries* [of CAKCHIQUEL (Coto, early seventeenth century), MATLALTZINCA (Basalenque 1642), and TZELTAL (Ara, possibly as early as 1571)].

The late seventeenth century produced a few more *grammars* [of CHIAPANEC (Albornoz 1691), CHOLTI (Morán 1695), QUICHÉ (Vico 1675?), Yucatec MAYA (San Buenaventura 1684), and ZOQUE (González 1672)] and *dictionaries* [of CAKCHIQUEL (Santo Domingo 1693) and QUICHÉ (Basseta 1698?)].

The mid eighteenth century produced a new wave of *grammars* [of CAKCHIQUEL (Ximénez 1722?), HUASTEC (Tapia 1767), MIXE (Quintana 1729), ÓPATA (Lombardo 1702), OTOMI (Neve y Molina 1767), POCOMAM (Morán 1720), POCOMCHI (Zúñiga 1720), QUICHÉ (Anleo 1744), TEPE- HUÁN (Rinaldini 1743), and TOTONAC (Zambrano 1752)] and *dictionaries* [of CAKCHIQUEL (Ximénez 1750?), CORA (Ortega 1732), QUICHÉ (Barrera 1745), and ZOQUE (Pozarenco 1733)].

The mid- and late-nineteenth century saw reprints of some of these earlier works and the late-nineteenth and early-twentieth the first beginnings of modern production: of *grammars* [of AMUZGO (Belmar 1901), CHATINO (Boas 1913), CHICHIMEC (Angulo 1933), CHOCHO (León 1911), CORA (Preuss 1932), HUICHOL (Diguet 1911), IXIL (Stoll 1887), KEKCHI (Stoll 1896), POCOMCHI (Stoll 1888), QUICHÉ (Schultze-Jena 1944), TEPECANO (Mason 1917), Tequistlatec CHONTAL (Belmar 1900), TLAPANEC (Radin 1933), and Yucatec MAYA (Tozzer 1921)]. Precursor of an interim trend is the paucity of *dictionaries* [CORA (Preuss 1935)] produced during this period.

Not until the mid-thirties of the present century did intensive study of a fuller range of descriptive linguistic foci through the full range of indigenous languages spoken in New Spain begin in earnest. William Cameron Townsend, after experience in Mexico with modern NAHUATL (Townsend 1935, 1945) and in Guatemala with modern CAKCHIQUEL (Townsend 1961), founded a Summer Institute of Linguistics whose purpose was to train Bible translators in the relevant skills (including the more purely descriptive linguistic ones). As these translators were trained, they were sent to the field, in Mexico and in Guatemala, to live with each group of Indians, to learn their language practically, to describe it scientifically, and to translate the scriptures into it inspirationally. Although these tasks were not always accomplished in this order, over the following forty years each individual language in the area was provided with at least a pair of practising linguists. By 1974, moreover, all major dialect variants of such languages were provided with such teams. Upwards of ninety languages and dialects are covered in this way at the present time.

The result has been a veritable flood of materials, descriptive or illustrative, of these languages and dialects: grammars, dictionaries, and texts. Upwards of a dozen complete *New Testaments* (Wares 1970) have been produced: CHINANTEC (Ojitlán 1968), CHOL (Tumbalá 1960), CHUH (San Sebastián Coatán 1969, San Mateo Ixtatán 1970), HUICHOL (1967), KANJOBAL (San Miguel Acatán 1960; Santa Eulalia-Barillas 1973), KEKCHI (1961), MAM (San Ildefonso Istahuacán 1968; San Juan Ostuncalco 1940), MAZATEC (1959), MIXTEC (San Miguel El Grande 1961), QUICHÉ (1946), TARASCAN (1969), TOTONAC (1959), TRIQUE (1968), Bachajón TZELTAL (1964), Oxchuc TZELTAL (1956), and ZOQUE (1967). Upwards of a dozen bilingual *dictionaries* have appeared: CHATINO (Pride 1970), Mayo CAHITA (Collard 1962), CORA (McMahon 1959), HUASTEC (Larsen 1955), KEKCHI (Sedat 1955), MIXE (Schoenhals

1965), MIXTEC (Dyk 1965), Tetelcingo NAHUATL (Brewer 1962), Zacapoaxtla NAHUAT (Key 1953), POPOLUCA (Clark 1960), SERI (Moser
1961), TARAHUMARA (Hilton 1959), Papantla TOTONAC (Aschmann
1973), Zapotitlán TOTONAC (ASCHMANN 1962), Oxchuc TZELTAL (Slocum
1953), Bachajón TZELTAL (Slocum 1965), TZOTZIL (Delgaty 1964).
Upwards of a dozen relatively full *grammars* have been published:
CHATINO (Pride 1965), Palantla CHINANTEC (Merrifield 1968), Quiotepec
CHINANTEC (Robbins 1968), Huamelultec CHONTAL (Waterhouse 1962,
1967), Tequistlatec CHONTAL (Turner 1967-68), HUICHOL (Grimes 1964),
Jicaltepec MIXTEC (Bradley 1970), Penoles MIXTEC (Daly 1973), Isthmus
NAHUAT (Law 1966), Tetelcingo NAHUATL (Pittman 1954), Zacapoaxtla
NAHUAT (Robinson 1966), Mezquital OTOMI (Hess 1968), Sierra POPO-
LUCA (Elson 1960), Northern TOTONAC (Reid 1968), Huistec TZOTZIL
(Cowan 1969), Isthmus ZAPOTEC (Pickett 1960, 1967), Mitla ZAPOTEC
(Briggs 1961), ZOQUE (Wonderly 1951-1952). Innumerable focussed
articles on phonology, morphology, and syntax of the upwards of 90
languages and dialects have appeared in an increasing variety of linguistic journals (Wares 1968, 1971). The quantity of material which has
appeared on (and in) the indigenous languages of Mexico and Guatemala
is disproportionately large, both in the earlier, and, increasingly so, in the
modern periods.

What may we say in particular characterization of these materials,
both of the earlier and of the modern periods?

The earlier descriptive materials follow the model of Antonio de
Nebrija's *Gramática Castellana* which first appeared, most auspiciously,
in 1492, as 'the companion of rule' – to use Nebrija's felicitous phrase.
Since Nebrija's grammar systematically compared the grammar of
contemporary Castilian Spanish with that of Latin, known to all the
priests, it served as a guide to the process of description which the
priests, not all of them native speakers of Spanish, would most naturally
follow, as they proceeded to learn the indigenous languages of New
Spain, and as they, in some instances, proceeded to teach Latin (and
Spanish) to some of the more gifted speakers of the indigenous languages. The model of Nebrija's *Gramática Castellana*, the first full grammatical treatment of any European vernacular, continued to be applied
to the indigenous vernaculars of New Spain, throughout the course of
Spanish empire, that is, from 1521 to 1821, a period of three hundred
years.

Conscientious and comprehensive, some of these grammars (such as
Carochi's *Arte de la lengua mexicana* [1645]) are still today excellent

examples of the art. All contain surprising points of detail which show that linguistic perceptiveness, with respect to phonetics, morphology, syntax, and semantics, is no recent attainment in the history of the science. All merit (and have not yet received) full critical edition and commentary (and recasting in accordance with the criteria of modern linguistics, in one or more of the more recent modes). Such restatement will inevitably shed light, not only on questions of modern descriptive theory, but perhaps even more importantly, on the history of the languages of contrast and comparison (Latin and Spanish), and on the contemporary statuses of indigenous and non-indigenous cultures and societies.

Permeating all these materials, both grammatical and lexical, both descriptive and textual, is an accounting, sometimes personal, sometimes ethnic, of the clash of cultures and societies, of the reconciliation, sometimes personal (as with Ixtlilxochitl 1891, 1892), sometimes ethnic (as with the Tlaxcaltecs, Gibson 1952), between different cultural traditions and different organizations of society, and of the increasing syncresis of Old and New Worlds – an accounting which might well furnish exemplars for the modern societies and cultures of present-day Middle America and for those of the rest of the modern world.

The quantity of 'classical' Middle American indigenous language texts material is great (that of CLASSICAL NAHUATL (Garibay 1953, 1954) is comparable to that of Classical Latin, that of CLASSICAL YUCATEC MAYA (Barrera 1949) to that of Classical Greek). Its quality, at best, compares not unfavorably with that of the Roman and Greek tradition. All of it furnishes precious information on and insight into the cultural and societal changes which have taken place over half a millenium of contact and contract, between millenia-old cultures and societies, indigenous to the Americas and alien to them, and some of it may provide partial paradigms for the on-going process of adjustment, between indigenous 'guests in the house' and alien occupiers of it, through which a more humanly equitable modus vivendi may eventually develop, and which might provide, to the rest of the world, a Middle American model for such development.

With the independence of Mexico and Central America from Spain in 1821, the doors were opened to other influences on the social, cultural, and linguistic process. The influence of the Catholic clerical model continued, but was now leavened by secular influences, from Europe (chiefly from France and from Germany), from the United States of North America (toward the end of the nineteenth and the beginning of the twentieth centuries), and by new clerical influences (Protestant, and, most recently, again, Catholic). Rémi Siméon's *Dictionnaire de la langue nahuatl* (1885), Otto Stoll's *Die Sprache der Ixil-Indianer* (1887), and Franz Boas' *Notes on the Chatino language of Mexico* (1913) are representative of the former. The flood of materials (Wares 1968, 1970, 1971), largely produced by the collaborators of the Summer Institute of Linguistics since the mid-thirties of the present century, are representative of the latter.

The (relatively) full grammars are couched in a variety of descriptive frames: those of Hart (1957, AMUZGO), Pride (1965, CHATINO), Merrifield (1968, Palantla CHINANTEC), Robbins (1968, Quiotepec CHINANTEC), Waterhouse (1962, 1967, Huamelultec CHONTAL), Turner (1967-68, Tequistlatec CHONTAL), Grimes (1964, HUICHOL), Bradley (1970, Jicaltepec MIXTEC), Law (1966, Isthmus NAHUAT), Robinson (1966, Zacapoaxtla NAHUAT), Hess (1968, Mezquital OTOMI), Mayers (1957, POCOMCHI), Elson (1960, Sierra POPOLUCA), Reid (1968, Northern TOTONAC), Cowan (1969, Huistán TZOTZIL), Pickett (1960, 1967, Isthmus ZAPOTEC), Briggs (1961, Mitla ZAPOTEC), and Wonderly (1951-52, ZOQUE) are framed, to a fairly large degree, in that version of Pike's (1954-60) tagmemic theory which immediately precedes their period of composition. An outgrowth and continuation of Bloomfield's (1933) grammatical theory, as presented in his *Language* and and exemplified in his later publications (such as his *The Menomini Language* 1962), tagmemic theory is neither, for long, uniform, nor, for better or for worse, hermetic – its practitioners participated in its formation and competing theories exerted their influence upon it. It is our good fortune that so large a variety of linguists, with such varied training, working on so large a variety of languages, have subjected any one grammatical theory for so long a period to such extensive testing. It is to be hoped that their experience will be the object of careful scrutiny by one of those non-partisan linguistic theorists, who, interested in the process of theory formation more than in the espousal of particular theories, may make an important contribution to the history of science by exploiting these rich descriptive linguistic materials.

It is likewise our good fortune that in some considerable number of cases other linguistic theories have been put to the test in the delineation of the features of other languages indigenous to New Spain. Louis Hjelmslev's (1961) glossematic theory was applied by Pittman (1954) to Tetelcingo NAHUATL and, fifteen years later, by Rasmussen (1969) to Todos Santos MAM. Morris Swadesh's linguistic theory as presented in his *La Nueva Filologia* (1941, second edition 1968) was applied by Cazés (1967) to Oxtotilpan MATLALTZINCA, by Manrique (1967) to Jiliapan PAME, and by Robles (1962) to Bachajón TZELTAL. More eclectic descriptive theories were applied by Johnson (1962) to Yaqui CAHITA, by Troike (1959) to COAHUILTEC, by Escalante (1962) to CUITLATEC, by Peck (1951) to Ostuncalco MAM, by Andrade (1957) and by Blair (1971) to Yucatec MAYA, by Croft (1951-54) to Matlapa and by Whorf (1946) to Milpa Alta NAHUATL, by the Fosters (1948) to Sierra POPOLUCA, by Mary Foster (1969) to Ichupio and by Paul Friedrich (1971, 1973) to 'San José Ocumicho – Cocucho' TARASCAN, by Kaufman (1971) to Aguacatenango TZELTAL and by Sarles (1966) to San Bartoleño TZOTZIL. Lounsbury's (1953; 1-24) theoretical stance is in part reflected in Fought's (1967) CHORTI, and McQuown's, in part, in Hopkins' (1967) CHUH and in Day's (1973) JACALTEC. Both Attinasi's (1973) CHOL and Furbee's (1974) TOJOLABAL reflect the influence of Chomsky's (1957, 1965) linguistic theories. Increasingly, further departures from any one of these linguistic theories are becoming manifest in the descriptive treatments of individual authors, as individual linguists become more restive within the confines of a particular theory. It is to be hoped that this restiveness is evidence of a new creativity in the on-going struggle to adapt the descriptive frame to the object of description. It is to be hoped, furthermore, that a linguistic theorist may be inspired, by the variety of these descriptive frames and by the richness of these descriptive materials, to draw up a natural history of linguistic theory formation which will make a further important contribution to the history of science. Of particular interest, in this connection, are those cases where more than one descriptive frame has served as a vehicle for the presentation of varieties of a single language: NAHUAT(L) as seen by Law (1966, Isthmus), by Croft (1951-54, Matlapa), by Whorf (1946, Milpa Alta), by Pittman (1954, Tetelcingo), and by Robinson (1966, Zacapoaxtla); TZOTZIL as seen by Sarles (1966, San Bartolomé de los Llanos), by Cowan (1969, Huistán), and by Colby (1963, Zinacantan); TARASCAN as seen by Foster (1969, Ichupio) and by Friedrich (1971, 1973, "San José Ocumicho – Cocucho"); and MAM as seen by Peck (1951, San Juan Ostuncalco) and by Rasmussen (1969, Todos Santos).

Of interest to the historian of science, too, is the comparison and contrast of the more diverse modern theories (Davis 1973) of linguistic description with the more uniform ancient theories: of Olmos' (1547), Rincón's (1595), and Carochi's (1645) presentations of CLASSICAL NAHUATL with that of Croft (1953) (in his Matlapa) or that of Newman

(1967) in the linguistics volume of the *Handbook of Middle American Indians*, that of Ximénez (1722?) of CLASSICAL QUICHÉ with that of Johannes Friedrich (1955) or that of Edmonson (1967) in the *Handbook*, that of Coronel (1620) of CLASSICAL YUCATEC with that of Barrera (1946) or that of McQuown (1967) in the *Handbook*. Of even greater interest, in this same connection, would be a comparison and contrast of a 'Classical' presentation of the grammar of a language still spoken today with one or more modern presentations of that same language: Olmos' (1545) CLASSICAL NAHUATL with Whorf's (1946) modern MILPA ALTA, Zambrano's (1752) mid-eighteenth century Hueytlalpan TOTONAC with McQuown's ([1940] 1971) mid-twentieth century COATEPEC, or Córdoba's (1578) CLASSICAL ZAPOTEC with Pickett's (1960) modern ISTHMUS or Briggs' (1961) modern MITLA. Half a millenium of application of a variety of linguistic theories to the description of the indigenous languages of New Spain affords a more than ample spectrum of exemplary cases on which to ground a general exposition of the development of descriptive linguistic theory. We trust that some linguist may soon be persuaded to undertake the task.

Parallel to the flood of modern descriptive grammars for the indigenous languages of New Spain, collections of texts (both original and translated), together with comprehensive dictionaries (both textually derived and *ad hoc* elicited) are appearing in increasing numbers. *Texts* in CHOL (Whittaker 1965), CHORTI (Fought 1972), CORA (Díaz 1945) MIXTEC (Dyk 1959), and POCOMCHI (Mayers 1958) have appeared in print, in HUASTEC (McQuown 1971) and MAM (Peck 1975), in NAHUAT (Law 1949) and in NAHUATL (Pittman 1949), in Yucatec MAYA (Vermont 1971), in QUICHÉ (Cochojil 1974) and in TOJOLABAL (Mendenhall 1949), in Coatepec TOTONAC (Oropeza 1971), in TZELTAL (Slocum 1949) and in TZOTZIL (Weathers 1949) on microfilm. Modern *dictionaries* in Mayo CAHITA (Collard 1962), Tataltepec CHATINO (Pride 1970), CORA (McMahon 1959), San Luis Potosí HUASTEC (Larsen 1955), HUAVE (Warkentin 1952), HUICHOL (McIntosh 1954), IXCATEC (Fernández 1961), JACALTEC (Day 1971), KEKCHI (Sedat 1955), MAM (McQuown 1975), MAZAHUA (Stewart 1954), MIXE (Schoenhals 1965), San Miguel el Grande (Dyk 1965) and Jamiltepec (Pensinger 1974), MIXTEC, in Gulf (Law 1949) and in Zacapoaxtla (Key 1953) NAHUAT, and in Tetelcingo NAHUATL (Brewer 1962), in Mezquital OTOMI (Wallis 1956), PAPAGO (Saxton 1969), Sayula POPOLUCA (Clark 1960), QUICHÉ (Xec 1954) (Wick 1975), SERI (Moser 1961) and TARAHUMARA (Hilton 1959), in Papantla (Aschmann 1973), in Xicotepec de Juárez (Reid 1974), and in Zapotitlán (Aschmann 1962)

TOTONAC, in Bachajón (Slocum 1965) and in Oxchuc (Slocum 1953) TZELTAL, in San Andrés (Delgaty 1964) and in Zinacantan (Laughlin 1968) TZOTZIL, in Isthmus (Pickett 1965) ZAPOTEC, and in ZOQUE (Harrison 1948) have appeared in print, in HUASTEC (McQuown 1975) and in MAM (McQuown 1975), in Yucatec MAYA (Blair 1975), in QUICHÉ (Wick 1975), in TOJOLABAL (Mendenhall 1949), and in Coatepec (McQuown 1975) TOTONAC on microfilm. These texts and these dictionaries cover the full range of the indigenous societies and cultures of New Spain, from the most primitive (such as the Seri, the Huave, or the Mixe) to the most cultivated (such as the Aztec, the Maya, or the Quiché). A comparison and contrast of the societal and cultural content of these textual and lexical materials now available in the languages of these societies and cultures will constitute an invaluable auxiliary to the anthropological investigation of these contemporary indigenous groups. In those cases where both modern and ancient (i.e. 'classical') materials on these languages, cultures, and societies are available, careful comparison and contrast of their contents will provide invaluable information on their pre- and post-Conquest contacts with other indigenous groups. A satisfying societal and cultural history of New Spain and of pre-Conquest Mesoamerica will not be written until such textual and lexical sources have been carefully exploited.

From the beginnings in the 1520's down to the on-going efforts of the present time, the concerns of the practitioners of the descriptive linguistic art have not been in the first instance scientific. From the start, the primary and most immediate concern has been (and for the most part still continues to be) for the forging of tools for spiritual and practical ends: for the creating and maintenance of empire, for the conversion to and administration of the faith, for the education in spiritual and practical arts of the faithful. Of the works produced on (and in) indigenous languages during the first century after the Conquest, eight out of ten were neither grammars nor dictionaries, but rather catechisms, breviaries, and translations of scriptural and exegetical materials, all these for the use of the clerical and lay ministers who were charged with the education and administration of the indigenous populations. The relative percentages of effort expended on the production of different types of indigenous language materials over the centuries may have varied slightly from time to time: Fray Bernardino de Sahagún ([1575-77] 1950-70) encouraged his Aztec informants to record their own oral literature and to describe in their own Nahuatl tongue their own culture and their own society, but it is only through fortunate accident and not through the intent of the clerical and lay administrators of the time that these materials have survived down to the present day; the organizers of modern efforts to utilize indigenous language materials for conversion, education, and administration have encouraged the production of New Testament translations, and of primers for initiating literacy, and readers for inculcating precepts of better health, better agriculture, better arts and crafts, in the first instance, and only rarely have individual workers strayed from the official norm by encouraging Indians to record their own oral traditions or to compose original literature in their own languages. The overwhelming majority of such materials has been prepared for the purpose of inducing the adoption or facilitating the imposition of non-Indian norms on Indian populations.

There are signs that this imbalance may be modifiable. The number of non-clerical linguists (Wauchope-McQuown 1967) is on the rise. In the first centuries after the Conquest, there were none. In the nineteenth and in the early twentieth centuries, small numbers of lay linguists, both domestic (Orozco y Berra 1864, Pimentel 1874-75) and foreign (Boas 1917, Brinton 1885, 1887, Mason 1917, Seler 1887, Siméon 1885, Stoll 1887, 1888, 1896) became involved in work in Mexico and Guatemala. Since the mid-thirties, the number of such individuals, domestic (González Casanova 1946 of Mexico, Schumann 1973 of Guatemala) and foreign (Whorf 1946, J. Friedrich 1955, Schoembs 1905, 1949, Schultze-Jena 1944, Andrade 1941, 1957, McQuown 1940, 1971, Swadesh 1969, Barlow 1949, Newman 1967, Foster 1948, 1969, Croft 1953, Zimmermann 1963, 1965) has continued to rise. During the last decade and a half, a half dozen a year have acquired vested interests in studies of Middle American languages, cultures, and societies. And, during the last few years, a few indigenous linguists (Xec [and Burgess] 1955, Álvarez 1970) have come to be concerned with the study and description of their own societies, cultures, and languages. Accompanying this trend has been the increasing production, on the one hand, of materials which incorporate a more self-conscious focus on problems of linguistic theory, and, on the other, of materials, originally composed in an indigenous language, whose content more directly reflects the society and culture of the speakers of that language.

There is, finally, some small indication that indigenous linguists, and indigenous writers in a more general sense, may become involved in direct composition and in skillful translation of materials which reflect the wider world, in its historical, scientific, and technological aspects, materials which may make directly available to the speakers of the indigenous languages of New Spain the facilities both for the reflection of their own societies and cultures and for the assimilation and adaptation of those aspects of other societies and cultures, which give them the option of wider integration should they choose to exercise it.

On all counts, then, from the perfecting of linguistic descriptive theory, through the use of such theory in presenting grammatical and lexical facts, to the presentation (in original or in translated form) of linguistic texts, to the exploitation of such texts for the light they shed on the societies and cultures of the people who compose them, both in their historical and in their contemporary aspects, to the provision of the linguistic means for wider cultural and societal integration (both internal and external), the indigenous societies of New Spain (with their cultures and languages) may yet furnish an even brighter exemplar of the 'Americanist contribution' to general linguistic, and to general cultural and societal studies.

University of Chicago

BIBLIOGRAPHY

Abbreviations

APSL	American Philosophical Society Library
BJGI	Biblioteca Joaquín García Icazbalceta
BLB	Bancroft Library, Berkeley
BML	British Museum Library (London)
BMNA	Biblioteca del Museo Nacional de Antropología (Mexico)
BNMa	Biblioteca Nacional (Madrid)
BNMx	Biblioteca Nacional (Mexico)
BNP	Bibliothèque Nationale (Paris)
BSMGE	Biblioteca de la Sociedad Mexicana de Geografía y Estadística
CEM	Centro de Estudios Mayas
CGLM	Coleccíon de gramáticas de la lengua mexicana
CIA XVI	Colección de Incunables Americanos, Siglo XVI
CVM	Cuadernos del Valle del Mezquital
ESGAASAK	Eduard Seler: Gesammelte Abhandlungen zur Amerikanischen Sprach- und Alterthumskunde. 5 vols. Berlin 1902-23.
FA	Fonds américain
ff.	folios
JCBL	John Carter Brown Library (Providence, Rhode Island)
LC	Library of Congress
MCM[(M)A]CA	Microfilm Collection of Manuscripts on [(Middle) American] Cultural Anthropology
Myn Stud	Mayan Studies

NL	Newberry Library (Chicago)
PUL	Princeton University Library
SI:ISA	Smithsonian Institution: Institute of Social Anthropology
TUL	Tulane University Library
UHAGAK: B(VkKGSpr)	Universität Hamburg: Abhandlungen aus dem Gebiet der Auslandskunde: Reihe B (Völkerkunde, Kulturgeschichte und Sprachen)
UNAM:BFLI	Universidad Nacional Autónoma de México: Biblioteca de Filología y Lingüística Indígenas
UPL	University of Pennsylvania Library
UV: BFFL	Universidad Veracruzana: Biblioteca de la Facultad de Filosofía y Letras
V	Viñaza

REFERENCES

Albornoz, J. de. 1691. Arte de la lengua chiapaneca..., 22 ff., Ms. [BNP:FA 38] [NL, photograph (44 pp.)].

Alvarado, F. de. 1593. Vocabulario en lengua misteca... (Tamaçulapa), Balli, México [BML 12910.cc.20. (pp. 10 + 204 ff.)] [NL, photograph (419 pp.)].

Álvarez, A., and K. Hale. 1970. Toward a manual of Papago grammar: Some phonological terms. International Journal of American Linguistics 36.83-97.

Andrade, M. J. 1957. A grammar of Modern Yucatec [-Maya], xiv + 462 pp. (typescript) [1941] [MCMCA Series VII Number 41].

Angulo, J. de. 1933. The Chichimeco language. International Journal of American Linguistics 7.152-94.

Anleo, B. 1744. Arte de la lengua quiche..., 67 ff., Ms.[copia] [BNP:FA 9], Panajachel, [NL, photograph (136 pp.)].

Ara, D. de. 1571. Vocabulario en lengua tzeldal [español-tzeltal], 164 ff., Ms, [UPL] [NL, photograph 328 pp.)].

—. 1571. Egregium opus... [+ Copanaguastla grammar] (pueblo de Taquin Vitz) [Tzeltal?], 167 pp. [sermons] + 40 pp. [grammar] + 5 pp. [index], Ms., [NL].

Aschmann, P. H. 1962. Vocabulario totonaco de la Sierra [Zapotitlán], 171 pp., Instituto Lingüístico de Verano, México.

Aschmann, P. H., and B. Aschmann. 1973. Diccionario totonaco de Papantla, 268 pp. Instituto Lingüístico de Verano, México.

Attinasi, J. 1973. Lak t'an (La palabra de nosotros) (A grammar of the Chol [Mayan] word), ca. 400 pp., Ph.D. thesis, University of Chicago, Chicago.

Barlow, R. H. 1949. The extent of the empire of the Culhua Mexica. Berkeley and Los Angeles: University of California Press. [Ibero-Americana 28].

Barrera, F. 1745. Vocabulario castellano-quiché...doctrina... confessionario. Ms. [NL, photograph, 201 pp.].

Barrera-Vásquez, A. 1946. La lengua maya de Yucatán. Edición Oficial del Gobierno de Yucatán, México. [Enciclopedia Yucatanense 6.205-92].

—, and S. G. Morley. 1949. The Maya chronicles. Washington, D.C.: The Carnegie Institution of Washington, Contributions to American Anthropology and History 10:48.1-85.

Basalenque, D. 1640. Arte de la lengua matlaltzinga..., 121 ff., Ms. [NL, photograph, 242 pp.]

—. 1642. Vocabulario...castellano...matla[lt]zinga..., ff. 1-40; 41-178, Ms. [V 177], [NL, photograph, 411 pp.]

—. 1642. Vocabulario...matlaltzinga...castellano..., ff. 123-242, Ms., [V 177], [NL, photograph, 286 pp.]

Basseta, D. de. 1689. Vocabulario quiché [Rabinal] [espagnol-quiché: ff. 1-160], Ms., [BNP:FA 59], [NL, photograph, 320 pp.]

—. 1698. Vocabulario quiché [Rabinal] [quiché-espagnol, ff. 161-239], Ms., [BNP:FA 59], [NL, photograph, 171 pp.]

Belmar, F. 1900. Estudio de el chontal ... fraseología, cuentos y vocabulario [tequistlateco] ... por Román Juárez, 372 pp., Oaxaca, [NL].

—. 1901. Investigación sobre el idioma amuzgo...vocabulario español-amuzgo..., 163 pp., Oaxaca, [NL].

Blair, R. W. 1971. Yucatec Maya phonology and morphology, vi + 146 pp. Chicago: University of Chicago [1964] [MCMCA Series XIX Number 109].

—, and R. Vermont-Salas. 1975. Yucatec-Maya-English vocabulary, 174 pp. Chicago: University of Chicago [1964], [MCMCA Series XXX Number 160].

—, and —. 1975. English-Yucatec-Maya vocabulary, 176 pp. Chicago: University of Chicago [MCMCA Series XXX Number 161].

Bloomfield, L. 1933. Language, ix + 564 pp. New York: H. Holt and Company.

—. 1962. The Menomini Language, xi + 515 pp. New Haven: Yale University Press.

Boas, F. 1913. Notes on the Chatino language of Mexico. American Anthropologist, n. s. 15.78-86.

—. 1917. El dialecto mexicano de Pochutla, Oaxaca. International Journal of American Linguistics 1.9-44.

Bradley, C. H. 1970. A linguistic sketch of Jicaltepec Mixtec, 97 pp., Summer Institute of Linguistics, University of Oklahoma, Norman, Summer Institute of Linguistics Publications 25.

Brewer, F., and J. G. Brewer. 1962. Vocabulario mexicano de Tetelcingo, 274 pp., Instituto Lingüístico de Verano, México.

Briggs, E. 1961. Mitla Zapotec grammar, iv + 110 pp., Centro de Investigaciones Antropológicas de México e Instituto Lingüístico de Verano, México.

Brinton D. G. 1885. The annals of the Cakchiquels [original text with a translation, notes and introduction], 234 pp., Philadelphia, Library of Aboriginal American Literature 6.

—. 1887. Ancient Nahuatl poetry [texts and translation, introduction, notes, and vocabulary], 177 pp., Philadelphia, Library of Aboriginal American Literature 7.

Carochi, H. 1645. Arte de la lengua mexicana, 275 pp., Ruiz, México, [NL], [BML 621.e.32 (132 fs.)], [LC:PM 4063.C 27 (6 + 132 ff.)].

Castro, A. de. 1542. Sermones en lengua matlaltzinga, 187 ff. Ms.

Cazés Menache, D. 1967. El pueblo matlaltzinga de San Francisco Oxtotilpan y su lengua, Instituto Nacional de Antropología e Historia, México, [Escuela Nacional de Antropología e Historia: Serie Antropológica: 2:III:2].

Cepeda, F. 1560. Artes de los idiomas chiapaneco, zoque, tzendal, y chinanteco, ff. [missing], México.

Chomsky, N. 1957. Syntactic structures. The Hague: Mouton.

—. 1965. Aspects of the theory of syntax. Cambridge: Massachusetts Institute of Technology Press.

Clark, L. 1961. Sayula Popoluca texts, 216 pp. Summer Institute of Linguistics, University of Oklahoma, Norman.

—, y N. D. de Clark. 1960. Vocabulario popoluca de Sayula, 165 pp. Instituto Lingüístico de Verano, México.

Cochojil-González, R. (transcr. and trnsl.). 1974. Quiché (Maya) texts (preliminary transcription and translation) [Chichicastenango], 784 pp. Chicago: University of Chicago [1935] [1964-71] [MCMCA Series XX Number 111].

Colby, L. M. 1963. Zinacantan Tzotzil sound and word structure, 130 pp., Ph.D. thesis. Cambridge: Harvard University.

Collard, H., y E. S. Collard. 1962. Vocabulario mayo [cáhita], 219 pp., Instituto Lingüístico de Verano, México.

Córdoba, J. de. 1578. Arte del idioma zapoteca, 304 pp., Morelia, Michoacán; 1886 [NL], reimpreso por Nicolás León.

—. 1578. Arte en lengua zapoteca..., 7 + 125 + 2 ff., [falto del folio 81?], Balli, México, [JCBL S13b/V176 R].

—. 1578. (ed. Wigberto Jiménez Moreno). Vocabulario castellano-zapoteco, [facsimile], México, 1942.

—. 1578. Vocabulario castellano-zapoteco, 227. pp., México, 1893 [NL], [JCBL S13b/ V 176 R.]

Coronel, J. de. 1620. Arte en lengua de maya..., 102 pp., Garrido, México, [NL, photograph] [TUL, photograph: 497.2055 C 822 Rare Book Case (106 pp.)]

Coto, T. Vocabulario de la lengua cakchiquel..., 955 pp., Ms. [APSL] [(early?)17th c. (?)] [NL, photograph]

Cowan, M. M. 1969. Tzotzil [Huistán] grammar, ix + 119 pp., Summer Institute of Linguistics, University of Oklahoma, Norman, Publication 18.

Croft, K. 1951. Pratical orthography for Matlapa Nahuatl. International Journal of American Linguistics 17.32-36.

—. 1953. Matlapa and Classical Nahuatl: With comparative notes on the two dialects, xvii + 122 pp., Ph. D. thesis, Bloomington: University of Indiana, [University Microfilms: Doctoral Dissertation Series: 5858]

—. 1953. Matlapa Nahuatl II: Affix list and morphophonemics. International Journal of American Linguistics 19.274-80.

—. 1954. Matlapa Nahuatl III: Morpheme arrangements. International Journal of American Linguistics 20.37-43.

Cruz, J. de la. 1571. Doctrina christiana en la lengua guasteca cõ la lengua castellana..., 52 ff., Ocharte, México, [JCBL S 13a/V 176 R] [Tulane University Library, photograph]

Daly, J. P. 1973. A generative syntax of Penoles Mixtec, 90 pp., Summer Institute of Linguistics, University of Oklahoma, Norman, Publication 42.

Davis P. W. 1973. Modern theories of language, xii + 404 pp., Englewood Cliffs: Prentice-Hall.

Day, C. C. 1971. Diccionario jacalteco-español: español-jacalteco, 22 pp. mimeo + 93 + 62 pp. computer printout; University of Rochester.

—. 1973. The Jacaltec language, viii + 135 pp., University of Indiana Publications, Bloomington/The Hague: Mouton.

Delgaty, C. C. 1964. Vocabulario tzotzil de San Andrés, ix + 81 pp., Instituto Lingüístico de Verano, México, Vocabularios Indígenas "Mariano Silva y Aceves" 10].

Díaz Flores, R. (introd. por R. H. Barlow), 1945. Textos en idioma cora, 24 pp., Escuela Nacional de Antropología e Historia Publications 3].

Diguet, L. 1911. Idioma huichol. Journal de la Sociéte des Américanistes de Paris 8.23-54.

Dyk, A. 1959. Mixteco texts, 248 pp., Summer Institute of Linguistics, University of Oklahoma, Norman, Publication 3.

—, y B. Stoudt. 1965. Vocabulario mixteco de San Miguel el Grande, 132 pp., Instituto Lingüístico de Verano, México.

Edmonson M. S. 1967. Classical Quiché. Handbook of Middle American Indians 5: Linguistics, ed. by R. Wauchope and N. McQuown, pp. 249-67.

Elson, B. 1960. Gramática del Popoluca de la Sierra, 133 pp., Universidad Veracruzana, Jalapa, [UV:BFFL 6].

Escalante, R. 1962. El cuitlateco, 59 pp., Departamento de Investigaciones Antropológicas, Instituto Nacional de Antropológia e Historia, México, Direcciôn de Investigaciones Antropológicas: Publicaciones, 9].

Feria, P. de. 1567. Doctrina cristiana en lengua castellana y çapoteca, 116 ff., Ocharte, México [BNMa].

Fernández, B. 1567. Doctrina mixteca, 184 ff., Ocharte, México, [BSMGE].

Fernandez de Miranda, M. T. 1961. Diccionario ixcateco: [esbozo de gramática]; ixcateco-español, español-ixcateco; textos; expresiones; palabras de origen español, 207 pp. Instituto Nacional de Antropología e Historia, México, Dirección de Investigaciones Antropológicas: Publicaciones, 7.

Foster, M. L., and G. M. Foster. 1948. Sierra Popoluca speech, iii + 45 pp. Government Printing Office, Washington D.C., SI:ISA 8.

Foster, M. L. 1969. The Tarascan language [Ichupio], xii + 200 pp. University of California Publications in Linguistics 56, Berkeley and Los Angeles.

Fought, J. G. 1967. Chortí (Mayan): Phonology, morphophonemics, and morphology, 247 pp., Ph.D. thesis. New Haven: Yale University; Ann Arbor: University Microfilms.

—. 1972. Chorti (Mayan) texts, 566 pp. Philadelphia: University of Pennsylvania Press, [Haney Foundation Series 51].

Friedrich, J. 1955. Kurze Grammatik der alten Quiché-Sprache im Popol Vuh, 143 pp. Wiesbaden: Steiner. [Akademie der Wissenschaften und der Literatur in Mainz: Abhandlungen der Geistes und Sozial Wissenschaftlichen Klasse 4.307-449.

Friedrich, P. W. 1971. The Tarascan suffixes of locative space: Meaning and morphotactics, 324 pp. Bloomington: Indiana University/The Hague: Mouton.

—. 1973. A phonology of Tarascan, vi + 232 + 8 pp. Chicago: University of Chicago, Department of Anthropology.

Furbee-Losee, N. L. 1974. The correct language: Tojolabal: A grammar with ethnographic notes, ca. 500 pp., Ph.D. thesis. Chicago: University of Chicago.

Gante, P. de. 1553. Doctrina cristiana en lengua mexicana, 8 + 164 ff., Juan Pablos, México, [BJGI].

Garibay Kintana, A. M. 1953. Historia de la literatura náhuatl: Primera Parte (Etapa autónoma: De c. 1430 a 1521), 507 pp., Porrúa, México.

—. 1954. Historia de la literatura náhuatl: Segunda Parte (El Trauma de la Conquista: 1521-1750), 429 pp., Porrúa, México.

Gibson, C. 1952. Tlaxcala in the sixteenth century, xvi + 300 pp. New Haven: Yale University Press.

Gilberti, M. 1558. Arte de lengua tarasca ó de Michoacán, 357 pp., Oficina Impresora del Timbre, México, [1558] 1898 [reimpreso por Nicolás León], [BML 12910.t.4] [344 pp.] [NL].

—. 1558. Arte en lengua de Mechoacán, 171 + 2 ff., Pablos, México, [BML C.38.c.54] [falta todo el pliego A, inclusa la portada].

—. 1559. Cartilla para los niños en lengua tarasca [y latín ó castellano], 20 ff., México, [ff. 12v - 32r en "Thesoro spiritual..." q. v.].

—. 1559. Diálogo de doctrina cristiana en la lengua de Mechuaca[n] ..., 610 pp., México, [NL].

—. 1559. Diccionario de la lengua tarasca ó de Michoacán, 518 pp., Oficina Impresora de Estampillas, México, 1901 [BML 12910. k.26.] [pp. 1-157 T-E; 159-173 verbos; 177-512 E-T; 513-516 adiciones].

—. 1559. Vocabulario en lengua de Mechuacan, 538 pp. [ff. 2-79 tarasco-español; ff 80-87 verbos [87 V en blanco]; ff. 2-180 español-tarasco], Pablos, México, [NL].

—. 1560. Evangelios en tarasco..., Ms., [missing].

—. 1575. Thesoro spiritual de pobres en lengua de Michuacán, 302 ff., Spinosa, México, (ff. 12v - 32r "Cartilla para los niños en lengua tarasca") [BML C. 36.b. 8.].

González, L. 1672. Arte breve y vocabulario de la lengua tzoque... de Tecpatlan, 41 + 293 pp. [1732 copy of], Ms., Tecpatlán, 1672 [BNP:FA 67] [NL, photograph (330 pp.)].

González Casanova, P. 1946. Cuentos indígenas (edición bilingüe nahuatl y española), viv + 202 pp., Imprenta Universitaria, México [UNAM:BFLI 1].

Grimes, J. E. 1964. Huichol syntax, 105 pp. The Hague: Mouton [Janua Linguarum: Series Practica 11].

Guevara M. de. 1638. Arte doctrinal ... para aprender la lengua matlalzinga..., [copie de Reinisch] 28 fs., Ms., [BNP:FM 409].

Harrison, W. R., and M. B. Harrison. 1948. Diccionario español-zoque, zoque-español, v + 85 + 85 pp., mimeo, Instituto Lingüístico de Verano, México.

Hart, H. L. 1957. Hierarchical structuring of Amuzgo grammar. International Journal of American Linguistics 23.141-64.

Hess, H. H. 1968. The syntactic structure of Mezquital Otomi, 159 pp. The Hague: Mouton [Janua Linguarum: Series Practica 43].

Hilton, K. S. 1959. Vocabulario Tarahumara, 216 pp. Instituto Lingüístico de Verano, México.

Hjelmslev, L. 1961. Prolegomena to a theory of language, 144 pp. (rev. ed.). Madison: University of Wisconsin Press.

Hopkins, N. A. 1967. The Chuj language, viii + 270 pp. mimeo. Austin: University of Texas, Department of Anthropology.

Ixtlilxochitl, F. de Alva. 1891. Relaciones (ed. by A. Chavero), México, [Obras Históricas 1].

—. 1892. Historia de la nación chichimeca (ed. by A. Chavero), México, [Obras Históricas 2].

Johnson, J. B. 1962. El idioma yaqui [cáhita], 303 pp. Departamento de Investigaciones Antropológicas, Instituto Nacional de Antropología e Historia, México, Direción de Investigaciones Antropológicos — Publicaciones, 10.

Kaufman, T. S. 1971. Tzeltal phonology and morphology, ix + 120 pp., Berkeley: University of California Publication in Linguistics 61.

Key, H., and M. R. Key. 1949. Puebla Sierra Aztec texts and dictionary, University of Chicago, [MCMCA Series V Number 27].

—. 1953. Vocabulario mejicano de la Sierra de Zacapoaxtla, Puebla, Mexico, 232 pp., Instituto Lingüístico de Verano, México.

Larsen, R. S. 1955. Vocabulario huasteco del Estado de San Luis Potosí, x + 208 pp, Instituto Lingüístico de Verano, México.

Laughlin, R. M. 1968. Tzotzil-English dictionary: Tzotzil-English: English-Tzotzil iii + 167 pp. computer printout; i + 134 pp. computer printout. Cambridge: Center for the Behavioral Sciences, Harvard University.

Law, H. W. 1949. Gulf Aztec texts and dictionary, pp. 556-707 in [MCMCA Series V Number 27]; Chicago: University of Chicago.

—. 1966. Obligatory constructions of Isthmus Nahuat grammar, 73 pp. The Hague: Mouton [Janua Linguarum: Series Práctica 29].

León, N. 1911. Vocabulario de la lengua popoloca, chocha y chuchona, 58 pp., Museo Nacional de Antropología, México, [1911] 1912 [Anales del Museo Nacional, (Mexico) 3a s. 3.1-48].

Lombardo, N. 1702. Arte de la lengua tequima llamada vulgarmente ópata, 472 pp., Ribera, México, [NL] [Ms.? [8 + 251 ff.) (Ramírez).

Lounsbury, R. G. 1953. Oneida verb morphology, 111 pp.; New Haven: Yale University Press Publications in Anthropology 48.

Manrique Castañeda, L. 1967. Jiliapan Pame. Handbook of Middle American Indians 5: Linguistics, ed. by R. Wauchope and N. McQuown, pp. 331-48. Austin: University of Texas Press.

Mason, J. A. 1917. Tepecano... . Annals of the New York Academy of Sciences 25. 309-416.

Mayers, M. K. 1957. Pocomchi verb structure. International Journal of American Linguistics 23.165-70.

—. 1958. Pocomchi texts with grammatical notes, 149 pp. Summer Institute of Linguistics, University of Oklahoma, Norman, Publication 2.

McIntosh, J. B., and J. E. Grimes. 1954. Niuqui 'Iquisicayari (vocabulario huichol-castellano, castellano-huichol), iv + 113 pp., Instituto Lingüístico de Verano, México.

McMahon, A., y M. A. de McMahon. 1959. Vocabulario cora, 193 pp., Instituto Lingüístico de Verano, México.

McQuown, N. A. 1933. Textos huastecos (transcritos y traducidos al español), 256 pp., University of Chicago, [1933] [1947-1948] 1971 [MCMCA Series XVII Number 103].

—. 1940. A grammar of the Totonac language, vii + 243 pp. [typescript], [1940] 1971 [MCMCA Series XVII Number 99].

—. 1941. Diccionario totonaco (totonaco-español) (español-totonaco), ca. 500 pp., University of Chicago, Chicago, [1941] [1955] [1971] 1975 [MCMCA Series XVII Number 101].

—. 1967. Classical Yucatec Maya. Handbook of Middle American Indians, 5 Linguistics, ed. by R. Wauchope and N. McQuown, pp. 201-47. Austin: University of Texas Press.

—. 1971. Diccionario huasteco (huasteco-español) (español-huasteco), ca. 500 pp., University of Chicago, Chicago, [1971] 1975 [MCMCA Series XVII Number 104].

—. 1971. Diccionario mame (mame-español) (español-mame), ca. 500 pp., University of Chicago, Chicago, [1971] 1975 [MCMCA Series XVI Number 107].

Mendenhall, C. D., and J. Supple, 1949. Tojolabal texts and dictionary, v + 60 + 156 pp. in MCMCA Series IV Number 26. Chicago: University of Chicago.

Merrifield, W. R. 1968. Palantla Chinantec grammar, 127 pp., Museo Nacional de Antropología, México, [Papeles de la Chinantla 5 Serie Científica 9].

Molina A. de. 1555. Aquí comiença un vocabulario en lengua castellana y mexicana ..., 532 pp., Pablos, México [NL] [BML C. 54.bb.20.] [fs. 1-261] [BNMx G-I-4-3; E.A.T.2.62].

—. 1571. Arte de la lengua mexicana y castellana, 1-4, 5-82 ff. 1ª parte]; 1-35 ff. [2ª parte], Ocharte, México [NL] [BML C.54. g.9] [BNMx G.I-4-4].

—. 1571. Vocabulario en lengua castellana y mexicana [4 + 121 + 2 ff.]; Vocabulario en lengua mexicana y castellana [2 + 162 ff.], Spinosa, México, [NL] [580 pp.] [LC PM 4066.M 72] [BML C.54.f.11; Case Book 7636].

—. 1571. Vocabulario en lengua castellana y mexicana... mexicana y castellana, 568 pp., [reimpreso en facsimile] Leipzig: Platzmann, [1571] 1880 [BML 12907.g. 12] [121 ff. + 162 ff.].

—. 1578. Doctrina christiana breue... en lengua mexicana..., México, 1546 [missing; reprinted in 1578 (?); 1675; 1718; 1732; 1735].

Morán F. 1685-95. Arte en lengua cholti...libro...confessionario...vocabulario, 182 pp., Ms., [NL, photograph].

Morán, P. de. 1720. Arte...de [la lengua pocomchi...por Fray Dionisio de Zúñiga...y traducido en la lengua pocoman de Amatitlán..., 9 ff. Ms., [NL, photograph (17 pp.)] [BNP:FA 53].

Moser, E., and M. B. Moser. 1961. Vocabulario seri-castellano, castellano-seri, ix + 199 pp., Instituto Lingüístico de Verano, México, [Vocabularios Indígenas "Mariano Silva y Aceves" 5].

Nebrija [Lebrija], E. A. de. 1492. Gramática castellana, [réproduction phototypique de l'édition princeps, 1492], Halle A. S., 1909.

—. 1492. Gramática de la lengua castellana [Salamanca, 1492], lxii + 272 pp.; New York: Oxford University Press, 1926.

Neve y Molina, L. de. 1767. Reglas de orthographia, diccionario, y arte del idioma othomí..., 184 pp. [NL], 160 pp. [BML 12907.a.35.], Bibliotheca Mexicana, México.

—. 1863. Reglas de orthographia, diccionario, y arte del idioma othomí..., 256 pp. [NL], 254 pp. [BML 12906.k.7.], Villanueva, México.

Newman, S. S. 1967. Classical Nahuatl. Handbook of Middle American Indians 5: Linguistics, ed. by R. Wauchope and N. McQuown, pp. 179-99. Austin: University of Texas Press.

New Testament [Chinantec] [Ojitlán] [Smith, P.]. 1968. Ju¹ Quie⁴ 'Më⁴ la² e² ca³jmo³ Tsa² chi¹⁻¹ quian¹⁻¹ jna'¹⁻¹ Jesucristo (El Nuevo Testamento de nuestro Señor Jesucristo), 1355 pp., Sociedad Bíblica de México.

New Testament [Chol] [Tumbalá] [Beekman, J.; Beekman, E.; Aulie, W.; Aulie E.; Anderson-Whittaker, A.; Warkentin, V.]. 1960. Jini tsiji'bʌt'an El Nuevo Testamento), 1224 pp., Sociedad Bíblica Americana, México.

New Testament [Chuj] [San Sebastián Coatán] [Williams, K.; Williams, B.]. 1969. A chañ Nuevo Testamento (Nuevo Testamento en Chuj: San Sebastián Coatán), 892 pp., Sociedad Bíblica en Guatemala, Guatemala.

New Testament [Chuj] [San Mateo Ixtatán]. 1970. A Ch'añ Nuevo Testamento Yic Viñ Cahal Jesucristo (Nuevo Testamento en Chuj de San Mateo Ixtatán), 1003 pp., Socidades Bíblicas en Guatemala, Guatemala.

New Testament [Huichol] [Grimes, J.; Grimes, B.]. 1967. Cacaüyari niuquieya xapayari türatu hecuame hepaüsita tati'aitüvame tasivicueisitüvame Quesusi Cürisitu mi'atüa (El Nuevo Testamento de Nuestro Señor y Salvador Jesucristo), 1319 pp., Sociedad Bíblica de México, México.

New Testament [Kanjobal] [San Miguel Acatán]. 1960. A Tx'an ac' Lajti' Yet Jajawil Jesucristo)([Nuevo Testamento en] Conob y Español), 822 pp., Sociedades Bíblicas en Guatemala, Guatemala, [1955] 1960.

New Testament [Kanjobal] [Santa Eulalia-Barillas]. 1973. A Tx'an Nuevo Testamento Yet Cham Jajawil K'anjobal [Conob], 1076 pp., Sociedades Bíblicas en Guatemala, Guatemala.

New Testament [Kekchi] [Sedat, W. (?)]. 1961. [Li Ac' Chak'rab] Li Ac' Testamento Re Li Kacua' Jesucristo (Tz'ibanbil li Santil Evangelio Chi Sa' Jo'cui'eb li Hu Tz'ibanbil Xbaneb Li Señor Jesucristo en Kekchi y Español), 1134 pp. + maps. Guatemala: Sociedad Bíblica Americana.

New Testament [Mam] [San Ildefonso Ixtahuacán] [Sywulka, E.]. 1966. Ju Ac'aj Tu'jil (El Nuevo Testamento de Nuestro Señor Jesucristo) (Versión Popular) (Mam de Huehuetenango y Español), 1277 pp.. Guatemala: Sociedad Bíblica en América Latina, [1966] 1968.

New Testament [Mam] [San Juan Ostuncalco] [Peck, D. M.]. 1940. Ju' Ac'aj Tu' jil Tu'n Kajau Jesucrist (Toj k.yol tuci'l Ac'aj Tu' jil toj Castiy), 310 pp. Nueba York: Sosiedad Te Biblia Toj Americ.

New Testament [Mazatec] [Cowan, F.; Pike, E.; Cowan, G.; Gudschinsky,

S.]. 1959. Xon^4-le^4 ni^{3}na^1 xi^3 t?a^{3}ts?e^4 Jesucristo (El Nuevo Testamento de Nuestro Señor Jesucristo), 1221 pp. Sociedad Bíblica Americana, México.

New Testament [Mixtec] [San Miguel el Grande] [partial] [Pike, K.; Stark, D.]. 1951. Testamento jaa maa jitoho-yo (El Nuevo Testamento de nuestro Señor Jesucristo), 365 pp., Tipográfica Indígena, Cuernavaca, 1951 [Jn 1957, 63 pp.; Ac 1960, 99 pp.; Jn 1, 2 and 3 Jn, 1967, 114 pp.].

New Testament [Quiché] [Burgess, D.] 1946. Ri Gkagk Testament Re Ri Ka Nim Ajawal Jesucrist (pa Ch'abal Quiché) (El Nuevo Testamento en Quiché), 310 pp. Gkagk York: Ri Sociedad Ajbibil American.

New Testament [Tarascan] [Lathrop, M.; Lathrop, E.]. 1969. Jimbaŋi Eiatsperakua Tata Jesukristueri (El Nuevo Testamento de Nuestro Señor Jesucristo), 916 pp.; Sociedad Bíblica de México, México.

New Testament [Totonac] [Zapotitlán] [Aschmann, H.]. 1959. Huã' xasãsti' xtalac-cãxlan nquin Tlãtica'n Jesucristo (El Nuevo Testamento), 1201 pp.; Sociedad Bíblica Americana, México.

New Testament [Trique] [San Andrés] [Longacre, R.]. 1968. Nguan$^{1-4}$ naca^5 nagui'-yaj^3 yya^3 yan'anj^{4}an nga^4 ne'^{2} (El Nuevo Testamento de nuestro Señor Jesucristo), 1633 pp.; Sociedad Bíblica de México, México.

New Testament [Tzeltal] [Bachajón] [Slocum, M.]. 1964. Yach'il Testamento (El Nuevo Testamento), 1262 pp.; Sociedades Bíblicas en América Latina, México.

New Testament [Tzeltal] [Oxchuc] [Slocum, M.]. 1956. Te ach' testamento yu'un te kajwaltik Jesukristoe (Nuevo Testamento), 1200 pp.; Nueva York: Sociedad Bíblica Americana.

New Testament [Zoque] [Copainalá] [Harrison, R.; Harrison, M.]. 1967. Te' JomepΛ Testamento (El Nuevo Testamento), 1412 pp., Sociedad Bíblica de México, México.

Olmos, A. de. Arte de lengua huasteca. [lost?]

—. Arte de lengua totonaca. [lost?]

—. 1547. Comiença el arte de la lengua mexicana..., fs. 20 R - 102 V, Ms., México, [BNMa 10081 Res. 165].

—. 1574. Arte y vocabulario en lengua mexicana, 576 pp., Ms., México [NL, photograph].

—. 1875. Grammaire de la langue nahuatl..., 291 pp., [Publiée par Siméon], Paris [NL].

—. 1885. Arte para aprender la lengua mexicana, 126 pp., Imprenta Nacional, México [NL], [reimpresión de la edición de Siméon] [CGLM 1 - 126].

Oropeza Castro, M. 1971. Textos totonacos [escritos en lengua materna por..., traducidos al español], 200 pp., [MCMCA Series XVI Number 100], [1939-1942] [1949-1950].

Orozco y Berra, M. 1864. Geografía de las lenguas y carta etnográfica de México, xiv + 392 pp. + map, Andrade y Escalante, México.

Ortega, J. de. 1732. Vocabulario en lengua castellana y cora..., [9 + 43 ff.], Lupercio, México, [NL 21, 90 pp.].

—. 1888. Vocabulario en lengua castellana y cora..., 92 pp., Tepic, [NL], [reimpreso por orden del General Leopoldo Ramana].

Peck, D. M. 1935. Textos mames (transcritos y traducidos por informantes nativos), ca 500 pp. Chicago: University of Chicago, [1935] [1950-1952] 1975 [MCMCA Series XVIII Number 106].

—. 1951. The formation of utterances in the Mam language [San Juan Ostuncalco], i + 164 pp., M.A. thesis; Hartford: Hartford Seminary Foundation.

Pensinger, B. 1974. Diccionario mixteco del este de Jamiltepec. Instituto Lingüístico de Verano, México.

Pickett, V. B. 1960. The grammatical hierarchy of Isthmus Zapotec, vi + 200 pp., Ph.D. thesis. Baltimore: University of Michigan, Linguistic Society of America. [Language Dissertations 56] [Language 36.1 (Pt. 2): 1-101 (Jan-Mar 1960)].

— (y colaboradores). 1965. Vocabulario zapoteco del Istmo, 163 pp. Instituto Lingüístico de Verano, México.

—. 1967. Isthmus Zapotec. Handbook of Middle American Indians 5: Linguistics, ed. by Wauchope and McQuown, pp. 291-310. Austin: University of Texas Press.

Pike, K. L. 1954-60. Language in relation to a unified theory of the structure of human behavior. Part I (1954), x + 170 pp.; Part II (1955), v + 85 pp.; Part III (1960), vii + 146 pp. Glendale: Summer Institute of Linguistics.

Pimentel, F. 1874-75. Cuadro descriptivo y comparativo de las lenguas indígenas de México (segunda edición única completa), 3 vols., Vol. 1, xvi + 426 pp., 1874; Vol. 2, 472 pp., 1875; Vol. 3, 570 pp., 1875. Epstein, México.

Pittman, R. S. 1949. Tetelcingo Aztec texts and dictionary. Chicago: University of Chicago, [MCMCA Series V Number 27].

—. 1954. A grammar of Tetelcingo (Morelos) Nahuatl, 67 pp. Baltimore: Linguistic Society of America, [Language Dissertations 50] [Language 30.1.2:1-67].

Pozarenco, J. 1733. Vocabulario de la lengua çoque, 354 pp., Ms., [JCBL], [NL, photograph].

Preuss, K. T. 1932. Grammatik der Cora-Sprache. International Journal of American Linguistics 7.1-84.

—. 1935. Wörterbuch Deutsch-Cora. International Journal of American Linguistics 8.79-102.

Pride, K. 1965. Chatino syntax ... [Tataltepec], 249 pp. Summer Institute of Linguistics, University of Oklahoma, Norman, Publication 12.

Pride, L., y K. Pride. 1970. Vocabulario chatino de Tataltepec, 103 pp. Instituto Lingüístico de Verano, México.

Quintana, A. de. 1729. Arte de la lengua mixe. Puebla [JCBL?].

—. 1891. Arte de la lengua mixe, 41 pp., [NL] [reimpreso por... Belmar] [JCBL?].

Radin, P. 1933. Notes of the Tlappanecan language of Guerrero. International Journal of American Linguistics 8.45-72.

Rasmussen Canger, U. 1969. Analysis, in outline, of Mam, a Mayan language, ix + 291 pp., Ph.D. thesis. Berkeley: Language Behavior Research Laboratory, University of California, Working paper 25.

Reid, A. A., and R. G. Bishop. 1974. Diccionario totonaco de Xicotepec de Juárez, 418 pp., Park Press.

—, —, E. M. Button, and R. E. Longacre. 1968. Totonac: From clause to discourse, 185 pp. Summer Institute of Linguistics, University of Oklahoma, Norman.

Reyes, A. de los. 1750. Arte en lengua mixteca ... Tepuzculula, 163 pp. Ortega, México [BML C.63.d.3.].

—. 1888. Arte en lengua mixteca (Balli/México/1593) [Tepuzculula], 96 pp. Paris: Klincksieck, [Actes de la Sociéte Philologique 18 (n.s. 3) 1888] [BML R.Ac. 9808 Vol. 18].

Rinaldini, B. 1743. Arte de la lengua tepeguana con vocabulario, confessionario, y catechismo..., 8 + 72 + 43 + 148 + 1 pp. Hogal, México [1745?] [NL (286 pp.)].

Rincón, A. del. 1595. Arte mexicana...vocabulario breve, [fs. 8 + 78 (arte) + 36 (vocabulario)] 206 pp., Balli, México [NL], [BML C. 58. a.10 (ff. 8 + 78 + 78V + 95 R)].

—. 1885. Arte mexicana..., 94 pp., Secretaría de Fomento, México [NL] [reimpreso por Peñafiel] [CGLM 225-280].

Robbins, F. E. 1968. Quiotepec Chinantec grammar, 150 pp., Museo Nacional de Antropología, México, [Papeles de la Chinantla 4, Serie Científica 8].

Robinson, D. F. 1966. Sierra Nahuat word structure, x + 166 pp. Hartford: Hartford Seminary Foundation [Hartford Studies in Linguistics 18], [Summer Institute of Linguistics Publications 22: Aztec Studies II, 186 pp.].

Robles-Uribe, C. 1962. Manual del tzeltal (gramática tzeltal de Bachajón), 115 pp., Universidad Iberoamericana, México, Publicaciones de Antropología: Lingüística 1].

Sahagun, B. de. 1575-77. Florentine Codex: General history of the things of New Spain [original Nahuatl text and English translation by A. J. O. Anderson and C. D. Dibble] Books 1-12, 1865 pp. Santa Fe/Salt Lake City: University of Utah and School of American Research, [1575-1577] 1950-1970.

San Buenaventura, J. de. 1684. Arte de la lengua maya..., 7 + 41 ff. [missing], Calderón, México.

—. 1888. Arte de la lengua maya..., 104 pp., 2nd ed., Mexico [NL], [reimpresa por Icazbalceta].

Santo Domingo, T. de. 1693. Vocabulario en la lengua cakchiquel y castellana, 139 ff., Ms., [BNP:FA 44] [NL, photograph (286 pp.)].

Sarles, H. B. 1966. A descriptive grammar of the Tzotzil language as spoken in San Bartolomé de los Llanos, Chiapas, Mexico, vii + 152 pp., Ph.D. thesis. Chicago: University of Chicago.

Saxton, D., and L. Saxton. 1969. Dictionary: Papago [and Pima] to English (O'odham-Mil-gahn); English to Papago [and Pima] (Mil-gahn-O'odham), 191 pp. Tucson: University of Arizona Press.

Schoembs, J. 1905. Material zur Sprache von Comalapa [Cakchiquel] in Guatemala, xi + 227 pp. Dortmund: Ruhfus. [TUL 497.204 S 364].

—. 1949. Aztekische Schriftsprache (mit Lautlehre), Text und Glossar, 212 pp. Heidelberg: Winter.

Schoenhals, A., y L. C. Schoenhals. 1965. Vocabulario mixe de Totontepec, 354 pp. Instituto Lingüístico de Verano, México.

Schultze-Jena, L. 1944. Popol Vuh. Das Heilige Buch der Quiché-Indianer von Guatemala, xx + 314 pp. Stuttgart und Berlin: Kohlhammer.

Schumann, O. 1973. La lengua chol, de Tila (Chiapas), 115 pp., Coordinación de Humanidades, Universidad Nacional Autónoma de México, México [CEM 8].

Sedat S., G. 1955. Nuevo diccionario de las lenguas K'ekchi' y española: K'ekchi'-español; español-k'ekchi', 273 pp., San Juan Chamelco, Alta Verapaz, Guatemala.

Seler, E. 1887. Das Konjugationssystem der Mayasprachen, Berlin [ESGAASAK 1.65-126].

Siméon, R. 1885. Dictionnaire de la langue nahuatl..., 2 + 75 + 1 + 710 pp., Imprimerie Nationale, Paris, [LC PM 4066.S 5].

Slocum, M. C. 1949. Tzeltal texts, microfilm. Summer Institute of Linguistics, México.

—. 1953. Vocabulario tzeltal-español [Oxchuc], 93 + 75 pp. Instituto Lingüístico de Verano, México.

—, y F. L. Gerdel. 1965. Vocabulario tzeltal de Bachajón, 216 pp. Instituto Lingüístico de Verano, México.

Stewart, D., S. G. de Steward, and H. Spotts. 1954. Vocabulario mazahua: mazahua-español, español-mazahua, 95 pp. mimeo. Instituto Lingüístico de Verano, México.

Stoll, O. 1887. Die Sprache der Ixil-Indianer (Ein Beitrag zur Ethnologie und Linguistik der Maya-Völker), x + 156 pp. Leipzig: Brockhaus, [NL].

—. 1888. [Die Maya-Sprachen der Pokom-Gruppe. Erster Theil:] Die Sprache der Pokonchi-Indianer, x + 203 pp. Wien: Hälder [NL].

—. 1896. [Die Maya-Sprachen der Pokom-Gruppe. Zweiter Teil:] Die Sprache der K'e'kchi-Indianer. Nebst einem Anhang: Die Uspanteca, vi + 221 pp. Leipzig: Köhler [NL].

Swadesh, M. 1968. La Nueva Filología, (con una biobibliografía del autor), 334 pp., 2nd ed. Editorial Libros de México, S. A., México.

—. 1969. Elementos del tarasco antiguo, 190 pp. Universidad Nacional Autónoma, México.

Tapia Zenteno, C. de. 1767. Noticia de la lengua huasteca..., 137 pp. Biblioteca Mexicana, México [NL].

Townsend, W. C. 1935. [Primer] [mexicano de Tetelcingo, Morelos] [1935], Tlaama-poaliz amoxtli, 14 pp., Mexicayotl, México, 1945.

—. 1961. Cakchiquel grammar, MynStud 1.1-79. Summer Institute of Linguistics, University of Oklahoma, Norman.

Tozzer, A. M. 1921. A Maya grammar (with bibliography and appraisement of the works noted) (Maya texts), 301 pp. Cambridge: Harvard University Press [NL] [Papers of the Peabody Museum of Harvard University 9].

Troike, R. 1959. A descriptive phonology and morphology of Coahuilteco, 148 pp., Ph.D. thesis, Austin: University of Texas.

Turner, P. 1966. Highland Chontal grammar. Ph.D. Dissertation, University of Chicago.

—. 1967. Highland Chontal phonemics. Anthropological Linguistics 9:4.26-32.

—. 1967. Highland Chontal phrase syntagmemes. International Journal of American Linguistics 33.282-86.

—. 1968. Highland Chontal clause syntagmemes. Linguistics 38.77-83.

—. 1968. Highland Chontal sentence syntagmemes. Linguistics 42.117-25.

Vargas, M. 1576. Doctrina christiana... en castellano, mexicano y otomi, ff. 1-23, 27... [incomplete]. Balli, México [BJGI].

Vermont-Salas, R. 1971. Yucatec Maya Texts (transcribed and translated into Spanish), 1428 pp. Chicago: University of Chicago, [1931-33] [1963-71] 1971 [MCMCA Series XIX Number 108].

Vico, D. de. 1675 (?). Arte de la lengua quiché o utlatecat; mode de ayudar a bien morir..., 35 ff. Ms., [BNP:FA 63] [NL photograph (69 pp.)].

Viñaza, C. M. y C. de la Manzano. 1892. Bibliografía española de lenguas indígenas de América, xv + 1 + 1 + 427 + 1 + 3 pp. Madrid: Sucesores de Rivadeneyra.

Wallis, E. E., and N. Lanier. 1956. Diccionario castellano-otomí, otomí-castellano, vii + 283 pp. Instituto Lingüístico de Verano, México, [CVM 1.1].

Wares, A. C. 1968. Bibligraphy of the Summer Institute of Linguistics 1935-68, xiv + 126 pp. Summer Institute of Linguistics, Santa Ana.

—. 1970. Bibliography of the Wycliffe Bible Translators, xxii + 84 pp. Wycliffe Bible Translators, Santa Ana.

—. 1971. Bibliography of the Summer Institute of Linguistics: Supplement No. 1, viii + 70 pp. Summer Institute of Linguistics, Santa Ana.

Warkentin, M., and C. Warkentin. 1952. Vocabulario huave: español-huave, huave-español, iv + 37 + 37 pp. Instituto Lingüístico de Verano, México.

Waterhouse, V. 1962. The grammatical structure of Oaxaca Chontal [Huamelultec], 121 pp., Ph.D. thesis, Ann Arbor: University of Michigan. International Journal of American Linguistics 28.2 (Part 2).

—. 1967. Huamelultec Chontal. Handbook of Middle American Indians, ed. by Wauchope and McQuown, pp. 349-67. Austin: University of Texas Press.

Wauchope, R. (general editor), N. A. McQuown (volume editor). 1967. Handbook of Middle American Indians, Volume 5: Linguistics, 402 pp. Austin: University of Texas Press.

Weathers, N. 1948. Tzotzil texts. [MCMCA Series IV Number 26, pp. iv + 157 + 215. Chicago: University of Chicago, [(Dec)1948] 1949.

Whittaker, A., and V. Warkentin. 1965. Chol texts on the supernatural, 171 pp. Summer Institute of Linguistics, University of Oklahoma, Norman, Publication 13.

Whorf, B. L. 1946. The Milpa Alta dialect of Aztec, with notes on the classical and Tepoztlan dialects. Linguistic Structures of Native America, ed. by H. Hoijer et al, pp. 367-97. Viking Fund Publications in Anthropology 6.

Wick, S. A., and R. Cochojil-González. 1975. English–Quiché-Maya vocabulary, 238 pp. Chicago: University of Chicago, [MCMCA Series XII Number 79].

—, and —. Quiché-Maya–English vocabulary, 238 pp. Chicago: University of Chicago, [MCMCA Séries XII Number 78].

Wonderly, W. L. 1951. Zoque I: Introduction and bibliography. International Journal of American Linguistics 17.1-9.

—. 1951. Zoque II: Phonemes and morphemes. International Journal of American Linguistics 17.105-23.

—. 1951. Zoque III: Morphological classes, affix lists, and verbs. International Journal of American Linguistics 17.137-62.

—. 1951. Zoque IV: Auxiliaries and nouns. International Journal of American Linguistics 17.235-51.

—. 1952. Zoque V: Other stem and word classes. International Journal of American Linguistics 18.35-48.

—. 1952. Zoque VI: Text. International Journal of American Linguistics 18.189-202.

Xec, P., and G. Maynard. 1954. Diccionario preliminar del idioma quiché: quiché-español, español-quiché, 152 + 55 pp. Instituto Bíblico Quiché, Quezaltenango.

Xec, P., and D. M. Burgess. 1955. Popol Wuj (Texto del R.P.F. [Francisco] Ximénez), xiii + 302 pp., El Noticiero Evangélico, Quezaltenango.

Ximénez, F. 1722 (?). Arte de las tres lenguas cakchiquel, quiché y tzutuhil...; tratado ...para la buena administración..., 362 pp., Ms., Santo Tomás Chichicastenango, [NL] [Ms. in the Newberry Library bound together with the Popol Vuh].

—. 1750 (?). Primera parte de el tesoro de las lenguas cakchiquel, quiché y tzutuhil, en que las dichas lenguas se traducen en la nuestra española, 430 pp., Ms., [NL, photograph].

Zimmermann, G. (ed. and transl.). 1963. Die Relationen Chimalpahin's zur Geschichte Mexico's: Teil 1: Die Zeit bis zur Conquista 152. [Aztekischer text], xv + 195 pp. Hamburg: Cram, De Gruyter, [UHAGAK 68:B (VKKGSpr):38].

—. 1965. Die Relationen Chimalpahin's zur Geschichte Mexico's: Teil 2: Das Jahrhundert nach der Conquista (1522-1615) [Aztekischer Text], v + 207 pp. Hamburg: Cram, De Gruyter, [UHAGAK 69:B (VKKGSpr): 39].

Zambrano Bonilla, J. 1752. Arte de lengua totonaca... [con oraciones y doctrina de la Sierra Baja da Naolingo, su author el Lic. D. Francisco Domínguez]..., 20 + 134 + 6 ff., Ortega, Puebla, [BML C.58.e.13.] [NL (234 pp.)].

Zúñiga, D. de. 1720. Arte...de la lengua pocomchi...[y traducido en la lengua pocoman...por F. P. de Morán], 9 ff. Ms., [BNP:FA 53] [NL, photograph (17 pp.)].

AMERICAN INDIAN LINGUISTICS
IN NEW SPAIN

DISCUSSION BY VIOLA WATERHOUSE

Professor McQuown is to be commended for his excellent survey of American Indian linguistics in New Spain from its inception 450 years ago to the present. Being basically a practitioner in this field and not a theoretician, I will content myself with adding a few grains to the impressive heap of information he has placed before us. These will primarily add further data about activity of the Summer Institute of Linguistics. My grains are in three piles: byproducts of American Indian linguistics in New Spain in terms of contributions to the basic teaching of linguistics, information about languages studied, and some specific recent publications of SIL.

American Indian linguistics in New Spain in the first 40 years was largely fostered by the patronage of Queen Isabella of Spain, who is now commemorated by the street named for her in downtown Mexico City. American Indian linguistics in New Spain in the last 40 years has been fostered and encouraged by the Linguistic Society of America, whose Golden Anniversary we are commemorating in this Symposium.

The first type of encouragement I would like to mention was through the LSA Linguistic Institutes. McQuown has mentioned the founding of the Summer Institute of Linguistics by Townsend. Kenneth Pike attended the second summer course of SIL and two years later went to the LSA Linguistic Institute at the University of Michigan. Through the stimulus he received there from Sapir, Bloomfield, Fries, Hockett, and others, he was encouraged in various aspects of his research. The results of this are seen in his current voluminous bibliography on a wide variety of topics, his continuing research and teaching at the University of Michigan, and his field guidance of young linguists, in process at present writing. Since his first attendance at the Linguistic Institute, some 35 or 40 other SIL field workers from Mexico and Guatemala (besides others from other fields) have profited from study there, and 25 or so of these have completed doctoral studies.

In the early years of the LSA, few universities offered courses in phonetics or in linguistics other than comparative Indo-European, and relatively few linguists were free to do field work. Even in 1947, when I attended the Linguistic Institute at the University of Michigan, linguists were complaining that the bulk of their time had to be spent in teaching basic courses in modern European languages. The summer Institutes, then, as well as the LSA meetings were an important source of stimulus for all sorts of theoretical discussion and development. These expanded in breadth and depth as more linguists were able to spend time in field work in New Spain and elsewhere. Their researches and those of our SIL field personnel have in turn contributed and enriched courses in various aspects of linguistic theory and practice at the LSA Institutes, at our SIL schools, and at universities such as Michigan, Indiana, Cornell, Chicago, Texas, and elsewhere, where some of us have had the privilege of teaching.

Our struggles, and those of others, to understand linguistic structures hitherto undescribed of languages hitherto unwritten, have contributed to the teaching of basic linguistic skills. Today's young linguists perhaps know little of the struggles we had to apply basic phonemic techniques in analyzing unwritten languages in order to provide a solid base for a practical alphabet. In the early days of SIL, the phonetics course occupied one side of an $8\frac{1}{2}$ by 11 sheet, and the phonemics the other. Problems encountered in complex phonological and grammatical systems, with their solutions, were eventually incorporated into our textbooks for the help and teaching of later generations of students. Thus our analytical techniques were first tested and refined in the field, then taught in our courses, and then described in textbooks – in that order.

In addition to training given and received by SIL personnel at LSA Institutes and at other universities, our own training program has expanded from the initial summer courses at the University of Oklahoma to include three others in the US and four others abroad, plus a year-round program at our SIL center in Dallas, affiliated with the University of Texas. A course for Japanese linguists is being prepared now to be taught next summer in Japan in Japanese. Some of our staff have also taught linguists and educators in courses offered by the Interamerican Program for Linguistics and Language Teaching (PILEI) in various academic centers in different parts of Latin America. We have also been able to help train young Mexican and Brazilian linguists at their national universities in Mexico and Brasilia, and in other courses in Mexico, as well as giving basic courses in linguistic and translation techniques to speakers of indigenous languages in the US, Philippines, Africa, New Guinea, and elsewhere. Our SIL field workers now number over 3,000 working in over 600 languages in 26 countries, and are recruited from 22 countries around the world. All these items are byproducts of American Indian linguistics in New Spain.

Turning now to languages studied and being studied, it is noteworthy that of the nine cited by McQuown as the first to be described, eight have modern grammars as well, seven have modern dictionaries, and seven have New Testaments. Five have published text material, either in print or in microfilm.

McQuown's listing shows that in the first 400 years (1524-1924) the total number of languages studied reached 31 (25 for Mexico, and 6 for Guatemala). In the 50 years since, a further 21 were added. The total studied in the past 50 years, including new items in languages studied in the first period, and in subvarieties of names listed for such languages, comes to 58, almost double that which was done in the first 400 years. This includes only full books, cited by McQuown from all sources. The current SIL bibliography, including only SIL materials, but items of all sizes, lists a total of 145 languages of New Spain. Some of these concern languages in which SIL does not contemplate a full field program. Current field work is in progress in 106 languages in Mexico and 19 in Guatemala.

Another phase of American Indian linguistics in New Spain, not mentioned by McQuown, is that of comparative studies of Mexican Indian languages. Monographs on Proto-Mixtecan (Longacre), Proto-Popotecan (Gudschinsky), and Proto-Chinantec phonology (Rensch) are in print, Proto-Otomanguean (Rensch) is is press, and Proto-Otopamean (Bartholomew), a University of Chicago dissertation, and Proto-Mazatec (Kirk) and Proto-Tepiman (Bascom), University of Washington dissertations, are available on microfilm. Mexican linguists Maria Teresa Fernandez de Miranda (before her death) and Jorge Suarez have worked on Proto-Zapotec. Their work has been hampered by the lack of data from crucial Zapotec languages, but this situation is now being remedied as further of these are now being studied.

Another area of current SIL production is that of practical grammars of indigenous languages, cast in the familiar mold of popular Spanish grammars. Work is in various stages of progress on Highland Oaxaca Chontal, Huave, Isthmus Nahuat, and Zoque, and on two varieties each of Mixtec, Otomi, and Zapotec.

A further area of recent focus, restricted to the state of Oaxaca, is that of the Archive of Indigenous Languages of Oaxaca, a government project. Materials for this have been prepared in Chatino, Chinantec, Chontal, Cuicatec, Huave, Mazatec, Mixe, Mixtec Trique, and two varieties of Zapotec. Descriptions are set up in comparable format, comprising a phonological statement, analyzed narrative and conversational texts (with tapes), an analyzed set of about 600 sentences and paradigms, and a small word list.

Turning to the matter of linguistic models cited by McQuown, it should be noted that the work on both the Mitla Zapotec and the Zoque were done before Pike's tagmemic materials were available. Also, the Palantla Chinantec and Tzotzil are not in the strict tagmemic tradition as set forth by Pike and Longacre, and the Jicaltepec Mixtec is primarily on a non-tagmemic model. It is to be hoped that someone will pick up McQuown's challenge to study the development of tagmemics and other theories in depth and to compare and contrast the various materials available. Contributions to this from the standpoint of tagmemics are Waterhouse (to appear), Brend (1973), and Pike and Brend (to appear).

Turning to recent SIL publications, I would like to comment on three areas: folklore, dialect testing, and native-authored material.

Text collections in individual languages have been mentioned by McQuown. Others have been produced in the form of concordances by the computer program of the University of Oklahoma. Individual texts have appeared in the Mexican journal *Tlalocan*. Now a volume of collected texts from 17 languages of Guatemala and Honduras has been published, edited by Mary Shaw. It is in two editions with identical cover and format, one in English and one in Spanish. The book is in three sections: a comparative discussion of salient motifs running through various texts and languages, free translations of the texts arranged alphabetically by native language names, and the native texts themselves with literal English or Spanish translation below. The format for the last section is that used in our SIL text series, with sentences numbered serially through a text, and words numbered through each sentence with the corresponding glosses correspondingly numbered. The orthography used is that used in other publications designed for speakers of the indigenous language.

The dialect testing program in progress for the past several years in Mexico and the techniques used have now been described in the volume *Dialect Intelligibility Testing* by Eugene Casad.

A final area of current activity in SIL field work is that of encouraging native-authored material. Many of our Indian colleagues are gifted in translation or lexicography or understanding of grammatical structure. Others show talent in creative writing in their own languages. In some recent field workshops, native authors from a number of language groups have not only written on a wide variety of subjects, but typed up their materials, cut stencils, run off, assembled and stapled pages to produce some very attractive books to take back to their villages. Some also show artistic talent and have illustrated their own books.

I will just mention three types of topics presented in these books. One is the preservation of priceless folklore items in danger of being lost as older story-tellers are dying off and the younger speakers are not learning to tell these tales. Some of our native authors are seeking to preserve such tales in print. A second type is practical material, for example on the use of compost or the treatment of parasites, or historical items such as the life of the great Mexican Indian patriot and statesman Benito Juarez. A speaker from the largely monolingual Lalana Chinantec group decided to translate a simple life of Juarez for his compatriots so that they could share the inspiration of the life of the lowly Zapotec shepherd boy who rose so high in both the history of his country and the esteem of his countrymen. A final type consists of familiar topics or items from one's own experience. A young Otomi teacher confined to a wheelchair has produced a lovely collection of simple stories, delightfully illustrated in part by herself. A group of Tila Chol school children wrote about house-building, tortilla making, preparation of cornfields and beanfields, and a trip taken to a neighboring village. A Mazahua, from a group whose members make frequent trips to nearby Mexico City, wrote from his own experience about the dangers of the road. This last is cleverly illustrated with examples of the kinds of things NOT to do in city or highway traffic.

It is to be hoped that in the future there will continue to be not only a flow of material by SIL authors and others describing language structures of New Spain in a variety of models, but also an increasing volume of books and articles by the speakers of those languages themselves on many topics of interest to themselves and to many others.

Summer Institute of Linguistics

REFERENCES

Brend, R. M., ed. 1973. Advances in tagmemics. North Holland Linguistics series 9.

Casad, E. 1973. Dialect intelligibility testing. Huntington Beach: Summer Institute of Linguistics.

Pike, K. L., and R. Brend, eds. To appear. The Summer Institute of Linguistics. Current Trends in Language Sciences, ed. by T. A. Sebeok. The Hague: Mouton.

—. To appear. Tagmemics. Current Trends in Language Sciences, ed. by T. A. Sebeok. The Hague: Mouton.

Shaw, M. A. 1971. According to our ancestors (Spanish edition: Segun nuestros antepasados). Huntington Beach: Summer Institute of Linguistics.

Wares, A. C. 1974. Bibliography of the Summer Institute of Linguistics 1935-1972. Huntington Beach: Summer Institute of Linguistics.

Waterhouse, V. G. To appear. The History and Development of Tagmemics (1956-1971). The Hague: Mouton.